STOUGH, Charlotte L. Greek Skepticism; a Study in Epistemology. *CHOICE*   *SEPT.'70*
Philosophy
California, 1969. 167p bibl 76-82464. 6.95
An excellent study of a movement of crucial importance for the understanding of Renaissance and early empiricist and rationalist philosophy (e.g. Hume's). Skeptics, reflecting on the view that we know
reality only indirectly through sense (which especially in Stoicism
favors the copy model), argued that since sense acquaints us with
appearances only and these are never logically *conclusive* reasons about
reality, we never do know it. Academic Skeptics (notably Carneades)
proposed that appearances can often *justify*, but never *guarantee*,
beliefs about the real; Pyrrhonists rejected all assertions about it, except
for those justifiable (and indubitable) ones merely about its appearances.
(Aenesidemus embraced phenomenalism while Sextus Empiricus asserted that nothing is really true, not even Skepticism!) A valuable
addition to the recent studies by Brochard and Hallie, and superseding
the older ones by Maccoll, Zeller, Patrick, Bevan, and Robin.
Stimulating, lucid, and presuming no knowledge of Greek, it can and
should be used by undergraduate students of epistemology, metaphysics, and the history of philosophy, e.g. with Popkin, *The History*

GREEK SKEPTICISM

CHOICE   *SEPT.'70*
Philosophy

of Scepticism from Erasmus to Descartes (1961; CHOICE, Jan. 1966),
Chisholm, *Theory of Knowledge* (CHOICE, Nov. 1966), and Wisdom,
"Metaphysics," in *Other Minds* (2nd ed.; CHOICE, July–August 1969).
Index

CHARLOTTE L. STOUGH is a member of
the Department of Philosophy at the University of California, Santa Barbara.

GREEK * * A STUDY IN EPISTEMOLOGY
SKEPTICISM

By CHARLOTTE L. STOUGH

UNIVERSITY OF CALIFORNIA PRESS

BERKELEY AND LOS ANGELES 1969

UNIVERSITY OF CALIFORNIA PRESS
BERKELEY AND LOS ANGELES, CALIFORNIA
University of California Press, Ltd.
London, England
Copyright © 1969 by The Regents of the University of California
Library of Congress Catalog Card Number: 76-82464
SBN 520-01604-1
Designed by Steve Reoutt
Printed in the United States of America

TO MY MOTHER AND FATHER

ACKNOWLEDGMENTS

I wish to express my gratitude to all those who have helped to make possible the writing of this book. I have benefited in countless ways from the ideas of colleagues and students on matters relating directly or indirectly to the subject of Greek Skepticism. It will be evident, moreover, that my manner of treatment owes much to Professor Benson Mates' work *Stoic Logic*, which has greatly influenced my thinking on the methods and practices of philosophical scholarship. More particularly, I am indebted to Professor Mates and to Professor W. Gerson Rabinowitz for valuable individual criticism of an earlier version of the manuscript. Their incisive comments resulted in numerous improvements in the final version of the text. Finally, I should like to express my appreciation to Miss Rona Sande, without whose painstaking editorial assistance this book could not have been brought to completion.

CONTENTS

ABBREVIATIONS

Ac.	Cicero, *Academica*
Dox.	Diels, *Doxographi Graeci*
Fin.	Cicero, *De Finibus*
M	Sextus Empiricus, *Adversus Mathematicos*
ND	Cicero, *De Natura Deorum*
PH	Sextus Empiricus, *Outlines of Pyrrhonism*
Poet.	Diels, *Poetarum Philosophorum Fragmenta*
Pr. Ev.	Eusebius, *Praeparatio Evangelica*
Subfig.	Galen, *Subfiguratio Empirica*
SVF	Von Arnim, *Stoicorum Veterum Fragmenta*
Vit.	Diogenes Laertius, *Vitae Philosophorum*
Vor.	Diels, *Fragmente der Vorsokratiker*

1 * INTRODUCTION

This book seeks to add dimension to our understanding of Greek Skepticism by concentrating attention on a particular area that is of philosophical interest to Skeptics and is both central to their movement and accessible to inquiry. The area to be explored includes those questions and problems broadly termed "epistemological," focusing on concepts such as knowledge, belief, experience, perception, sensation, and the like. The inquiry is aimed at combining historical accuracy with philosophical relevance, and to this end, an attempt is made to set the claims and arguments of Skeptics in the context of philosophical problems of paramount interest in the Hellenistic period. When the questions to which Skeptics addressed themselves are elicited, their views emerge, not as self-contained bodies of doctrine to be set alongside of and measured against competing "systems" of Greek philosophy, but rather as significant attempts to come to terms with perplexing problems connected with knowledge — problems of no less interest to philosophers today than to their ancient predecessors. Seen in this light the Skeptic arguments form the substance of a coherent and penetrating epistemological criticism, which can be examined for its import and explored for its philosophical implications.

To clarify these objectives it will be helpful to mention other possible approaches to the study of Greek Skepticism, different from the present one and useful in their own right. It is not the main task of this work to provide a general survey of skeptical doctrines or a history of those ideas in the ancient world. The accom-

1

plishments of historians in these areas[1] require to be complemented, it would seem, rather than duplicated. The limitations imposed here thus necessitate omitting a number of subjects of marginal interest which are dealt with, at least briefly, in these more general accounts — for example, both the critical discussions by Academic Skeptics of theological and moral questions and many of the diverse issues of varying philosophical importance found in the writings of Sextus Empiricus. If generality and completeness are sacrificed, however, a work on the epistemology of Skepticism is free to concentrate in greater depth on a systematic exposition and discussion of particular doctrines that, in an important sense, seem to define Skepticism but cannot be either sufficiently clarified or justly appreciated in a more general treatment of the subject. Another line of investigation, which has proven to be fruitful[2] but which we shall not attempt to discuss, concerns the influence of the classical Skeptics on modern thought. Many ties, both historical and philosophical, link the ancient Skeptics to modern thinkers, but a discussion of these affinities would inevitably change the character of an inquiry devoted primarily to the task of shedding light on the ancient doctrines, upon an adequate understanding of which, in any event, such comparative studies must ultimately rest. It is hoped that this book will stimulate discussion of the Greek Skeptics as well as further our appreciation of the complexities of philosophical skepticism.

GENERAL REMARKS

The philosophers with whom we are concerned are commonly classified by historians as either Pyrrhonists or Academic Skeptics. This classification, which differentiates Skeptics who claimed allegiance to Pyrrho from

[1] For an excellent and readable history of Greek Skepticism see Victor Brochard, *Les Sceptiques Grecs* (2d ed.; Paris, 1959).

[2] See Richard Popkin, *The History of Scepticism from Erasmus to Descartes* (Assen, 1960), which establishes a connection between Pyrrhonism and early modern thought through the manuscripts of Sextus Empiricus.

those belonging to the New Academy, indicates the two major branches of Greek Skepticism. The division is a useful one, but it does not signify two "schools" of Skepticism, each with a single body of doctrine defended by its members. For this reason, and because the information available allows us to examine the views of some Skeptics in considerably more detail than others, our investigation is divided into four principal sections: early Pyrrhonists (fourth and third centuries B.C.), Academic Skeptics (third and second centuries B.C.), Aenesidemus (possibly first century B.C.), and Sextus Empiricus (second and third centuries A.D.). The most important sources of information on these philosophers are Sextus Empiricus, Diogenes Laertius, Cicero, Eusebius, and Photius. Additional bits of information are scattered through the writings of other ancient authors.

Despite the fact that we are dealing with different skeptical philosophies that evolved over a long period of time, with no established "school" to unify them, we can give a rough characterization of the Skeptic movement to provide a context within which to set our inquiry. First, a word about the term "skeptic." Its etymology suggests no more than that a skeptic was an "inquirer."[3] It is not entirely clear when this term was first used as a title to identify the followers of Pyrrho or philosophers of the New Academy. But we do know that the tradition began in antiquity and seems to have originated with the Skeptics themselves, who apparently adopted the verb σκέπτεσθαι to characterize their movement. There is evidence that the corresponding noun σκεπτικοί (skeptics) was employed in a similar way even as early as Pyrrho's disciple Timon.[4] Subsequently, the term came to be applied with increasing frequency to both Pyrrhonists and Academics, establishing a tradition

---

[3] The word is derived from σκέπτεσθαι, which means "to observe carefully," "to examine," "to consider."

[4] Timon is said to have referred to Arcesilaus the Academic as σκεπτικός. Cf. *Poet.*, frag. 55. The term σκεπτοσύνη occurs in fragment 59 and ἄσκοπος in fragment 5.

that was followed by historians and is continued to this day.[5]

It is possible to pick out at least three features common to the Greek skeptical philosophies: first, their practical orientation; second, the denial of knowledge (or certainty); third, the resultant practice of suspending judgment. Both Pyrrhonists and Academics adopted a practical view of the nature and purpose of philosophizing, placing its value in the extent to which it influences the activity of life and furthers well-being. Pyrrhonists believed the ultimate good to be a state of psychic quietude (ataraxia) and accordingly justified philosophy as a means to this end. Academics, though they did not specify ataraxia as the end, set their philosophical inquiries in a practical context, justifying them by their efficacy in producing happiness. The eudaemonistic character, however, is more prominent at the outset of the movement (for which Pyrrho's moral influence seems to have provided a vital impetus) than it was subsequently as the interest of Skeptics gradually shifted from the ethical ground or justification of philosophy to the more intricate epistemological questions surrounding their negative stance with respect to knowledge. But the practical orientation of Skepticism never disappeared completely. Pyrrhonists consistently referred to their teachings as a way of life or movement (ἀγωγή), and the concern of all Skeptics with the relation of philosophy to ordinary life led them to look for workable solutions to problems unearthed by their own epistemological criticism. This study concentrates mainly on the Skeptic denial of knowledge and issues closely related to this, which together constitute the most important link between the various Greek skeptical philosophies. It is concerned, in particular, with exploring

---

[5] The ancients themselves were not in complete agreement over the title. Sextus Empiricus declines to call the New Academy "Skeptic" on the ground that Academics, despite their claims to the contrary, make "dogmatic" philosophical assertions. *PH*, I, 1–4, 13, 226.

the meaning of claims made by the Skeptics, inquiring into their justification of these claims, and examining their varying responses to the negative conclusions concerning knowledge.

HISTORICAL SKETCH

Historically Greek Skepticism spans a period of about six centuries, but it is doubtful whether it had a continuous existence from Pyrrho to Sextus Empiricus. It appears to have consisted of a series of sporadic but related movements, which flourished temporarily only to decline and be revived again before dying out completely. Pyrrhonism, for example, seems to have become quiescent soon after the death of Pyrrho's disciple Timon until Aenesidemus gave it new life, possibly in the first century B.C. It is also possible that there was a period of inactivity after the lifetime of Aenesidemus and before Sextus Empiricus. The period of Academic Skepticism, on the other hand, began during the lifetime of Timon and seems not to have lasted long after the death of its greatest exponent, Carneades. A brief sketch of the history of the movement will help to place this investigation in perspective.[6]

EARLY PYRRHONISM. It is generally agreed that the beginnings are to be located in the teachings of Pyrrho of Elis (*ca.* 365–275 B.C.). Later Skeptics, such as Aenesidemus and Sextus Empiricus, claim him as the founder of their philosophies and give his name to the Skeptic movement. Little is known of the philosophical ideas of Pyrrho. He is said to have been influenced by the Megarian and Democritean schools and by his travels to India with Alexander the Great. But he did not write down any account of his ideas, which have survived only as quoted or otherwise mentioned in various fragments of

---

[6] Unless otherwise mentioned, the account that follows is based on Eduard Zeller, *Die Philosophie der Griechen*, Vol. III (5th ed.; Leipzig, 1922), and Brochard, *op. cit.*

the writings of his pupil, Timon (*ca.* 325–235 B.C.). Pyrrho apparently was chiefly a moralist whose teachings embodied a way of life rather than a systematic philosophy.[7] He recommended a life of simplicity, placing no value in theoretical discussion and seeking only to attain ataraxia, which he deemed to be the highest good. His disciple Timon was a literary man by profession and the author of numerous satirical poems and plays. Fragments of his writings have been preserved in the form of quotations in the works of other ancient authors. Timon was not the head of any philosophic school following Pyrrho's death, nor is there evidence that he formally transmitted a set of doctrines to successors. Nevertheless, passages in the surviving fragments indicate that the early Pyrrhonists deserve credit for setting forth certain epistemological problems that later Skeptics took to be central to their own investigations.

ACADEMIC SKEPTICISM. The skeptical movement begun by Pyrrho in the fourth century was furthered in the New Academy under the leadership of Arcesilaus (315–240 B.C.) and Carneades (214–129 B.C.). Yet the Academic philosophy is not a continuation or elaboration of Pyrrho's views so much as a second version of Skepticism. The skeptical period of Academic thought during the third and second centuries seems to have been the product of a complex set of circumstances.

Academic Skeptics did not trace their origins to Pyrrho but apparently saw themselves as carrying on the tradition of the Old Academy of Plato. The Academic philosophy underwent a gradual transformation under Plato's successors. Plato's own views had been modified substantially by Speusippus and Xenocrates, and after

---

[7] Cicero, who does not take Pyrrho seriously as a philosopher, speaks of him as a moralist only. Cf. *Fin.*, II, 35, 43; III, 12, 43; V, 23. Since Pyrrho did not formally head a school of philosophy and, moreover, Cicero's Academic source Clitomachus preceded the revival of Pyrrhonism, Cicero does not treat Pyrrho as the founder of Greek Skepticism, as has since become customary.

the ascendancy of these men there is no evidence of Academic distinction in the area of mathematics. In the fourth and third centuries philosophers of the Academy, along with those belonging to other schools, became increasingly more interested in questions relating to ethics and the conduct of life. The declining interest in theoretical research is illustrated by the recommendation of Polemo, who followed Xenocrates as head of the Academy, that philosophers concern themselves with facts rather than theories.[8] The very probable influence of Pyrrhonism on Academic thought also has to be taken into account. Our information indicates that Arcesilaus and Timon were acquaintances and that a fair amount of rivalry existed between Pyrrhonists and Academics.[9] The likelihood of mutual influence is strengthened by the similarities between the two skeptical philosophies. Academics emphasized the practical foundation of their philosophical inquiries and the importance of suspending judgment.[10] But unlike the early Pyrrhonists, they cultivated a kind of dialectic virtuosity to induce suspense of judgment. Arguing artfully and persuasively on both sides of a question, they attempted to show that contradictory positions were equally defensible.[11] Neither Arcesilaus nor Carneades wrote down his philosophy, but both taught by lecture and debate. The doctrines of Carneades were recorded by his pupil Clitomachus, whose work was later consulted by Cicero when he wrote the *Academica*. Even the influence of Pyrrhonism, however, is not sufficient to explain the rapid growth of

[8] *Vit.*, IV, 18.

[9] *Vit.*, IX, 114, 115; IV, 33; Numenius in *Pr. Ev.*, XIV, 5, 729c–730b; *Poet.*, frags. 34, 35.

[10] *M*, VII, 158, 166. The Academic term, subsequently employed by all Skeptics, for suspense of judgment is ἐποχή. It is doubtful whether the early Pyrrhonists used ἐποχή in this technical sense, though the occurrence of ἐπεῖχε in one of the fragments of Timon (*Poet.*, frag. 63) makes this question problematic. See P. Couissin, "L'Origine et l'evolution de ἐποχή." *Revue des Etudes Grecques*, 42 (1929), 373–397.

[11] *Vit.*, IV, 28, 63; Numenius in *Pr. Ev.*, XIV, 6, 730b–c; XIV, 7, 736d; *Ac.*, I, 45; II, 60; *Fin.*, III, 41; *ND*, I, 11; *M*, IX, 1.

Academic Skepticism in the third and second centuries. It would be difficult to overestimate the significance of the Stoic philosophy in providing an impetus for the expansion of Skepticism during that period. The impact of this school, founded by Zeno of Citium early in the third century and carried on by Chrysippus, lasted well beyond the lifetime of Carneades. The fact that Arcesilaus and Carneades both directed their criticism toward Stoic theories is testimony to the influence of those doctrines. Clearly the philosophical battles waged between Stoics and Academics encouraged an elaboration and refinement of the Skeptic position that would have been unlikely under less stimulating conditions.[12] As a consequence, the philosophy of the Academics (and a substantial amount of what succeeding Skeptics had to say) is in many respects an answer to Stoicism.

Following the ascendancy of Carneades and his disciple Clitomachus, Academic Skepticism declined and was never again distinguished by an important thinker. Carneades' successors, Philo of Larissa and Antiochus of Ascalon, modified his doctrine to such an extent that it became almost indistinguishable from Stoicism. Nevertheless, the Skeptic movement did not die out. It merely migrated from Plato's Academy to Alexandria, where a renewed interest in Pyrrhonism began to manifest itself.

AENESIDEMUS. Aenesidemus is the most enigmatic of all the philosophers associated with the Skeptic movement. We know almost nothing about his life, and his philosophy, as it has come down to us, is marked by paradox.

The first problem concerns the exact period when Aenesidemus lived. It is impossible to fix his dates with any confidence. The judgments of historians vary by as much as two hundred years, beginning as early as 80 B.C. and ending around A.D. 130. Roughly the estimates of his *floruit* fall into three groups:[13] (1) 80–60 B.C. This

---

[12] Carneades says (*Vit.*, IV, 62): εἰ μὴ γὰρ ἦν Χρύσιππος, οὐκ ἂν ἦν ἐγώ.

[13] The following estimates are defended respectively by (1)

guess makes Aenesidemus a contemporary of Cicero,
Philo of Larissa, and Antiochus of Ascalon. It is supported by evidence from the testimony of Photius, according to whom: a) Aenesidemus complained that the
Academy of his period was contaminated by Stoicism[14]
(the Academic philosophy criticized conforms to what
we know of the doctrine of Philo of Larissa);[15] b) Aenesidemus dedicated one of his works to a certain Roman
named "L. Tubero"[16] (a contemporary of Cicero, also
called "Tubero," is mentioned by the former in his
writings). (2) Beginning of the Christian era. This later
estimate rests on the fact that Aenesidemus himself is
never mentioned by Cicero. If they were contemporaries,
Cicero's silence is difficult to explain, especially in view
of his more than passing interest in Skepticism. (3) A.D.
130. Aristocles, who lived at the end of the second cen-
tury A.D., refers to Aenesidemus as a recent ($\dot{\epsilon}\chi\theta\grave{\epsilon}s$ $\kappa\alpha\grave{\iota}$ $\pi\rho\acute{\omega}\eta\nu$)
philosopher in Alexandria,[17] which may indicate a later
date than the two mentioned above. But all we can really
determine from the above is that Aenesidemus lived
sometime between 80 B.C. and around A.D. 130, that he
lived and taught in Alexandria, and that he was dis-
satisfied with the eclectic character of the Academy of
his time, which was heavily influenced by Stoicism.

The philosophical views of Aenesidemus, as well as
the dates, are matters for conjecture. On the basis of
testimony from Photius, Diogenes Laertius, and Sextus
Empiricus there is every justification for classifying him
as a Skeptic. He apparently thought of himself as a
Pyrrhonist, since two of the five books he is said to have
written are entitled *Pyrrhonic Arguments* and *Outline
of Pyrrhonism*. Diogenes Laertius depicts him as defend-

Brochard, *op. cit.*, III, chap. 2; (2) Zeller, *op. cit.*, III, chap. 2,
p. 11; (3) Norman Maccoll, *The Greek Skeptics* (London and
Cambridge, 1869), pp. 68–69.

[14] Photius, *Bibliotheca*, Cod. 212, 170a14 (Berlin, 1824).

[15] *Ibid.*, 170a17; *PH*, I, 235; *Ac.*, II, 18.

[16] Photius, *op. cit.*, 169b32.

[17] Aristocles in *Pr. Ev.*, XIV, 18, 763d.

ing Pyrrho and maintaining, together with Timon, that the end (τέλος) is suspense of judgment, accompanied by ataraxia.[18] His arguments were designed to bring this about by showing that incompatible philosophical positions are equally plausible, hence, equally conjectural. In contrast with this evidence, however, is the puzzling statement of Sextus Empiricus that Aenesidemus regarded Skepticism as a way to the Heraclitean philosophy.[19] As Sextus goes on to explain, the view that the same thing appears to have opposite qualities is only a step away from what he describes as the Heraclitean view that opposites really do belong to the same subject. Though for the most part respectful of Aenesidemus, Sextus takes issue with him on this point and treats him on a par with the rest of the misguided theorists. Elsewhere he attributes to Aenesidemus some rather strange "Heraclitean" doctrines concerning the intellect and the unity of time, body, and being.[20] It is difficult to reconcile this last testimony with the supposition that Aenesidemus was a Skeptic. Perhaps the wisest course is to try to distinguish the critical aspect of Aenesidemus' thought from what are alleged to be his Heraclitean views. In any event, he can be considered a Skeptic only in regard to the former, and it is just this part of his philosophy that has survived. In this study, therefore, we shall examine only the skeptical side of Aenesidemus' thought and leave to one side all references to his more esoteric doctrines.

The progress of Skepticism during the period immediately following the death of Aenesidemus is obscure. His successors, with the exception of a certain Agrippa, are known to us only by name.[21] Agrippa attracted con-

---

[18] *Vit.*, IX, 62, 106, 107. Aristocles (*op. cit.*, XIV, 18, 758d), however, says that Aenesidemus held that the end was pleasure. But this statement is contradicted by Photius (*op. cit.*, 170b31).
[19] *PH*, I, 210.
[20] *PH*, III, 138; *M*, VII, 349–350; IX, 337; X, 216–218, 230–233.
[21] *Vit.*, IX, 116. Agrippa's dates are unknown. Cf. Brochard, *op. cit.*, III, chaps. 1, 6.

siderable attention as a Skeptic and as the author of five Tropes.[22] But since these arguments add nothing new to the epistemology of Greek Skepticism, they are not included in this study. Designed to furnish the Skeptic with a set of logical tactics to be employed in refuting arguments, they are simply more sophisticated weapons to induce suspense of judgment.

SEXTUS EMPIRICUS. The last and most prominent of the Skeptics is Sextus Empiricus. A Greek and a physician by profession, he lived sometime during the period between A.D. 150 and 250, but it is not certain where he was born or where he taught. Three works of Sextus have come down to us. The *Outlines of Pyrrhonism* constitutes a summary of Skepticism and an attack on alternative philosophies. The remaining two works, commonly referred to under the single title *Against the Mathematicians*, contain for the most part more elaborate versions of the arguments in the *Outlines*. A book on medicine and a work on the soul have not survived. The extant writings are valuable both as a source for Sextus' own views and for the information they contain on the history of Skepticism and other philosophical systems.

Sextus is perhaps the only important Skeptic who was also a physician, but the connection is not just one of chance. Long before his time the Pyrrhonic philosophy had become linked with medicine through a group of physicians known as "Empirics."[23] It is known that they were sympathetic with Pyrrhonism, and some may even

[22] *Vit.*, IX, 88–90; *PH*, I, 164–178. These Tropes consist in (1) citing a variety of conflicting beliefs about the matter in question, (2) forcing one's opponent into an infinite regress, (3) pointing out that nothing is apprehended except in relation to other things, (4) calling attention to unproven assumptions, (5) calling attention to circular reasoning.

[23] The following brief account of the Empirical school of medicine rests on Karl Deichgräber's *Die Griechische Empirikerschule* (Berlin, 1930). See also Brochard, *op. cit.*, III, chap. 1; IV, chaps. 1–3.

have considered themselves philosophical Skeptics.[24] The movement seems to have originated as early as 250 B.C. with a certain Philinus of Cos, in reaction to the doctrines of his teacher Herophilus, and to have continued until sometime well into the third century A.D. Some of the doctrines of these Empirics have been preserved in the writings of Galen and other sources.[25]

The Empirical physicians combated the "Dogmatic" medical theories of the schools of Herophilus and Erasistratus, which purported to explain the nature and causes of disease by postulating such entities as humors, atoms, and vital or animal spirits. Empirics, on the other hand, dismissed this sort of theory as speculative and avoided referring to unobservable entities in their own etiologies. They centered their researches into the causes and cure of disease in the study of observable symptoms. In fact, an illness or disease was regarded as a concurrence of symptoms (συνδρομὴ συμπτωμάτων).[26] They boasted an empirical methodology founded on observation (αὐτοψία, τήρησις), including facts observed by contemporaries or recorded by medical predecessors (ἱστορία), and inference from these observations. They sought insight into the nature of little understood diseases by noting, whenever possible, similarities and differences between these and other better known diseases. On the basis of these observed resemblances (between the symptoms of the known and unknown ailments, their respective physical

---

[24] Deichgräber (*op. cit.*) lists, together with fragments pertaining to their medical doctrines, the following among the Empirical physicians: Ptolemy of Cyrene (*ca.* 100 B.C.), Heraclides of Tarent (*ca.* 75 B.C.), a certain Zeuxis (beginning of the Christian era), Menodotus of Nicomedia (*ca.* A.D. 125), Theodas of Laodicea (*ca.* A.D. 125), and Sextus Empiricus (*ca.* A.D. 150–250).

Diogenes Laertius (*Vit.*, IX, 115–116) cites the following, among others, as Pyrrhonists: Ptolemy of Cyrene, a certain Heraclides (the teacher of Aenesidemus), a certain Zeuxis, Menodotus of Nicomedia, Theodas of Laodicea, and Sextus Empiricus.

[25] Especially important is *Subfig., passim* (Deichgräber, *op. cit.*). Cf. R. Walzer, *Galen on Medical Experience, passim* (London, New York, Toronto, 1944).

[26] *Subfig.* 45 (Deichgräber, pp. 56–57).

locations, and the sufferer's responses to remedies), they attempted to diagnose and treat the illness in question.[27] This inductive method (ἡ τοῦ ὁμοίου μετάβασις), given considerable precision by Menodotus and Theodas, was aimed at getting results of practical significance with no concern for theoretical speculation.

An attitude similar to the Pyrrhonic Skeptic is embodied in the principles of the Empirical physicians. At the inception of the medical movement the chief representatives of the Skeptic philosophy had been — or were — Pyrrho and Timon. Certain ideas associated with the Pyrrhonic philosophy became the model adopted by these physicians as a guide for both professional and personal life.[28] The Skeptic influence continued throughout the history of the Empirical school, thereby establishing a close link between the Pyrrhonic philosophy and medical research and practice. It is likely that there was a mutual exchange of ideas, the medics applying Skeptic principles in their scientific investigations and Pyrrhonists drawing on the results of the physicians. The similarity between the Empirical method of Menodotus and Theodas and the implications of Pyrrhonist epistemology tends to bear out this relationship. We find further that the Empirical medics even stated their method in the language of the great philosophical issue of the time. Observation (αὐτοψία, ἱστορία) was said to be the criterion of truth.[29] In spite of this close connection, however, it would be mistaken to suppose that Pyrrhonism as a philosophic movement ever became indistinguishable from the Empirical school of medicine. Sextus Empiricus, whose name suggests, perhaps mistakenly, that he belonged to the latter,[30] is particularly careful to distinguish them. In fact, he even claims that a certain "Methodic" approach to medicine is more consistent

---

[27] *Ibid.*, 36, 39, 54 (Deichgräber, pp. 44, 48, 69–70).
[28] *Ibid.*, 62, 64 (Deichgräber, pp. 82–84).
[29] *Ibid.*, 51–53 (Deichgräber, pp. 67–69).
[30] See also Deichgräber, frags. 6–9, pp. 40–41.

with Pyrrhonic Skepticism than the Empirical movement.[31] Physicians representing the various schools (Dogmatic, Empiric, Methodic) undoubtedly debated philosophic issues related to their discipline, but none of these
schools was identical with Pyrrhonic Skepticism.

Philosophically Sextus is an outspoken disciple of
Pyrrho. His debt to Pyrrho is evident in his statements
of the objectives of the Skeptic movement, in which he
emphasizes the importance of suspending judgment as
a means of attaining ataraxia.[32] The Skeptic, Sextus tells
us, is committed to no "dogma," which ranks him with
Pyrrho and sets him apart from the traditional philosophical schools.[33] Unlike Pyrrho, however, the Skeptic
of Sextus' era was concerned with justifying his position
by arguing against the theories of philosophers and ex-
posing their fallacies. The later Pyrrhonist allowed himself all the means at the philosopher's disposal to refute
any theory proposed.[34] Thus we find a large proportion
of Sextus' writings devoted to detailed philosophical
criticism, including arguments ranging from the most
subtle and perceptive to the obviously specious. But
Sextus, by no means deceived by his own sophistry,
justifies these arguments on uniquely pragmatic grounds.
The dogmatic philosopher is like a man afflicted with
illness — his most urgent need is to be cured. The Skeptic
undertakes the cure of philosophic disorders, just as a
physician provides a remedy for physical ailments.[35] The
remedy is justified by its success in restoring the patient
to health, and a logically weak argument on occasion
may bring about the desired cure. Sextus' penchant for

---

[31] *PH*, I, 236–241.

[32] *PH*, I, 8, 10, 25–27. Sextus qualifies the Pyrrhonic position
as follows. Ataraxia is the end with regard to δόξα, whereas modera-
tion (μετριοπάθεια) is the end with respect to affections beyond
one's control, e.g., hunger, thirst. *PH*, I, 29–30; *M*, XI, 147–150.

[33] *PH*, I, 1–4, 13.

[34] *PH*, I, 31: ἀντιτίθεμεν δὲ ἢ φαινόμενα φαινομένοις ἢ νοούμενα
νοουμένοις ἢ ἐναλλάξ.

[35] *PH*, III, 280–281.

philosophical argument is a fortunate accident for the student of Skepticism. His elaborate criticism enables us to fill out in considerable detail what would otherwise be a very fragmentary picture of the doctrines of Greek Skeptics.

2 * EARLY PYRRHONISM

Pyrrho of Elis, the originator of the Skeptic movement, is unfortunately the most inaccessible to the student of Skepticism. His name is surrounded by legend, much of it probably unreliable, and little material has come down to us concerning his ideas. For information of a philosophical rather than biographical nature, we must rely for the most part on often cryptic fragments from the poetic writings of his pupil Timon.[1] For this reason, all accounts of Pyrrho's ideas rest heavily on interpretation, and conclusions about his "philosophy" can have no more than a provisional character or significance. Yet the surviving fragments are worth noting, because they are suggestive of lines of thought adopted and elaborated, sometimes in considerable detail, by later Skeptics. This chapter, therefore, in which the germinal ideas of Greek Skepticism are located in the fragments and explored briefly for their implications, constitutes mainly, in accordance with the above caveat, a preface to the discussion of Skeptic doctrines that are found in succeeding chapters.

Of the surviving references in the literature to Pyrrho's philosophy, there is one account, reportedly a summary by Timon of Pyrrho's views, which is relatively straightforward and complete. This summary is therefore a good place to begin our inquiry. Following quotation of the passage, in which Pyrrho raises and answers three philo-

---

[1] The scant information on early Pyrrhonism necessitates treating the views of Pyrrho and Timon as a unit. Since Pyrrho left none of his ideas in writing, Timon has traditionally been considered his spokesman. Sextus Empiricus (*M*, I, 53) calls him the προφήτης τῶν Πύρρωνος λόγων.

sophical questions, each of the three topics mentioned
is examined individually along with other relevant fragments of Timon.

> His (Pyrrho's) pupil Timon says that the man who is to be
> truly happy must pay regard to these three questions: (1)
> What is the nature of things? (2) What attitude ought we
> to adopt with respect to them? (3) What will be the net
> result for those so disposed? He says that he (Pyrrho) de-
> clared that things are by nature equally indeterminable,
> admitting of neither measurement nor discrimination. For
> this reason, our sense experiences and beliefs are neither
> true nor false. Therefore, we ought not to put our trust in
> them, but be without beliefs, disinclined to take a stand
> one way or the other; and we should be steadfast in this
> attitude, saying about each thing individually that it no
> more is than is not, than both is and is not, than neither is
> nor is not. For those who are indeed disposed in this man-
> ner, according to Timon, there will result first, a disincli-
> nation to make assertions and then, ataraxia.[2]

NATURE OF THINGS

The context in which Pyrrho's three questions are asked
is worth noticing. It is a practical one; the stated goal is
well-being, and theoretical philosophy is conceived to
arise within that framework. The passage suggests that
the end of happiness dictates a certain manner of living,
part of which consists in the proper sort of philosophical
activity, and this involves consideration of the three
questions set forth in Pyrrho's statement.

SKEPTICISM AND PHILOSOPHICAL INQUIRY. The first question
to which the seeker of well-being is advised to address
himself is, "What is the nature of things?"[3] And to this
very general query Pyrrho supplies a predictably unspe-
cific answer, when he says of the world that it is "indeter-

---

[2] Aristocles in *Pr. Ev.*, XIV, 18, 758c–d (*Poet.*, chap. 9, pp. 175–
176). Unless otherwise mentioned, translations in this book are
my own.

[3] ποῖα πέφυκε τὰ πράγματα;

minable, admitting of neither measurement nor discrimination."⁴ An examination of Pyrrho's reply will
help to shed light on the nature of his question, the
clarification of which is the first step in an effort to
understand the character of his philosophical enterprise.

Commentary. The assertion that things are by nature
"indeterminable" (ἀδιάφορα) allows more than one interpretation. The predicate could be used descriptively,
implying that the character of anything to which it is
applied is indistinct or not sharply differentiated from
anything else. That is, Pyrrho could be asserting that the
world is really ("by nature") homogeneous, with the result that no components can be discriminated or distinguished one from another. It is not likely, however, that
he intended this since his next statement is that our sense
experiences (αἰσθήσεις) and beliefs (δόξαι), in which we
make such distinctions, are neither true nor false. Hence
the predicate "indeterminable" is probably not meant
to be descriptive of items in the world, but to say something about the relation between these entities and a
knowing subject, namely, that the properties of objects,
whatever they may be, cannot be discerned or discriminated (ἀστάθμητα καὶ ἀνεπίκριτα).⁵ In short, the nature of
things cannot be known. Thus we have at the very outset
a statement of Pyrrho's skepticism. Now if the remark
in question is not intended to inform us of an important
feature of the real world but to raise a question about

---

⁴ τὰ μὲν οὖν πράγματά φησιν αὐτὸν ἀποφαίνειν ἐπ᾽ ἴσης ἀδιάφορα καὶ
ἀστάθμητα καὶ ἀνεπίκριτα.

⁵ The predicates ἀστάθμητα and ἀνεπίκριτα are very likely ex-
egetical of ἀδιάφορα. The last term was used by the early Stoics in
an ethical context to apply to entities that were neither good nor
bad, but "indifferent," i.e., those which did not affect (or ought
not to have affected) an agent either positively or negatively, or
those toward which he was (or ought to have been) neutral. In
this passage the word has a similar, though extended, use. *All*
things are "indifferent," i.e., we ought neither to affirm (accept)
nor deny (reject) them, but remain neutral for the reasons sup-
plied by ἀστάθμητα and ἀνεπίκριτα. Sextus gives the full Stoic definition at *PH*, III, 177.

(cast doubt upon) our ability to know its character, it looks as if the original question about the "nature" of things is not a request for information, which could be satisfied by looking more closely at the objects in experience, measuring their properties more precisely, and citing the results of these investigations. The question is apparently intended to invite reflection instead of observation — in particular, reflection on the nature and limits of knowledge. Pyrrho's inquiry into the nature of things seems to be a philosophical rather than factual inquiry.

TRUTH AND FALSITY. Following his assertion that the nature of things is unknowable Pyrrho concludes that "for this reason our sense experiences and beliefs are neither true nor false."[6] Let us consider this statement in relation to the previous one.

Commentary. If the character of the world is unknown, it would seem to follow that the truth or falsity of our sense experiences (αἰσθήσεις)[7] and our beliefs (δόξαι) about the world is also unknown. Now on this basis it is tempting to suppose Pyrrho would have held that though some experiences and beliefs in fact are true and others false, we are never in a position to know which is the case, because the reality to which they refer eludes our grasp. This may indeed be the gist of Pyrrho's statement; but if the passage is read more strictly, a significantly different conclusion follows. What Pyrrho actually says is not that sense experiences and beliefs cannot be known to be true or false, but that they are in fact neither true nor false.[8] If we take his statement at face value, the implication is that experiences and beliefs are neither true nor false, because they cannot be established or known to be

---

[6] διὰ τοῦτο μήτε τὰς αἰσθήσεις ἡμῶν μήτε τὰς δόξας ἀληθεύειν ἢ ψεύδεσθαι.

[7] The ambiguity of "sense experiences" is also present in αἰσθήσεις, which is not technical and has no more precise a meaning than the English translation.

[8] This position was also held by Sextus Empiricus some six centuries later. See chap. 5.

true or false. Pyrrho's words seem to imply that verifiability[9] is a necessary condition of truth.

Alternately, we can explore the implications of the same assertion by asking what conditions would have to obtain for sense experiences and beliefs to be true or false. The only clue to an answer here lies in what appears to be Pyrrho's reason for denying their truth or falsity, namely, that the nature of things cannot be known. Let us imagine, then, contrary to hypothesis, that the character of the world *is* known. If this were the case, could we then say that sense experiences and beliefs are true or false? The answer is obvious, for under these circumstances they could be checked against the appropriate objects (or facts). Suppose, for example, someone knows that an object, which happens at the moment to be in his visual field, is yellow. His visual experience and his belief that it is yellow are therefore true, since they can be matched against the object whose color is already known. Implicit in the passage before us is the notion of a relation that holds between experiences (beliefs) and objects (facts) in the world and is analogous to that between a likeness (copy) and its original. A true experience or belief is one that can be determined to represent or conform to its object. But, says Pyrrho, no sense experiences or beliefs, therefore, are true or false, because they cannot be checked against the objects they are assumed to copy to establish their agreement or disagreement.

APPEARANCE AND REALITY. Let us go back now to Pyrrho's question about the nature of things and to his skeptical reply. Noting the verb "is by nature" (πέφυκε) in particular, we may compare his words in that context with a fragment from Timon's work, *On the Senses.*

---

[9] Though it sounds odd to speak of "verifying" data of sense, this is justified in the present context by the fact that "sense experiences" are said to be "neither true nor false." The implication is that we ought to be able to compare them with their objects to establish their truth.

I do not assert that honey (really) is sweet,
but that it appears (sweet) I grant.[10]

Commentary. The contrast here between "is" (ἔστι)
and "appears" (φαίνεται) suggests that in Pyrrho's original
question "is by nature" is meant to mark the same distinction between things as they are by nature and things
as they appear to us. His reply accordingly places the
former outside the limits of knowledge. Similarly, in
the fragment just quoted we can see that by declining to
say that honey really is sweet, Timon is in effect acknowledging ignorance of the nature of honey. But he does
not claim ignorance of the way it tastes, for he is willing
to grant that honey appears sweet regardless of its real
character. The opposition in these lines can be brought
out by the following pair of statements: (1) "Honey is
sweet," and (2) "Honey appears sweet." The first assertion makes a claim about a perceptual object (honey),
whereas the second is a report of someone's experience —
of that same item as it is experienced by someone. For
convenience let us call (1) a "perceptual statement" and
(2) a "sense statement." Statement (2) is acceptable to
Timon, but (1) is not. His reasons for rejecting (1) are
fairly clear from what has already been determined. The
real nature of things is unknown, so that the reports of
sense cannot be relied upon to give a true account of
their properties. Sweetness is experienced as a property
of honey, but because experiences of this sort are neither
true nor false, we cannot affirm that honey really is sweet.
The sense statement, however, makes no claim about the
properties of an object as they may exist independently
of what we experience. It does not commit the speaker
to a belief about the nature of honey. Statement (2), since
it is about the experienced property of the object, is
prima facie verifiable (confirmable), and this may account for its acceptability.

---

[10] Poet., frag. 74: τὸ μέλι ὅτι ἔστι γλυκὺ οὐ τίθημι, τὸ δ' ὅτι φαίνεται
ὁμολογῶ. Cf. *PH*, I, 20.

But the sense statement can be construed in more than one way. Consider the following alternative translations.

(2a) "Honey appears sweet to me (now)."

(2b) "Honey appears sweet to all (or most) persons." Statement (2a) refers uniquely to the present experience of the subject, whereas (2b) extends to the experience of others. This feature lends an air of certainty to (2a) that does not accompany (2b). Of course, the first assertion (unless construed as vacuously true) can be false. Its truth is contingent on the memory of previous experiences, recognition of the present experience as of a certain type, and a correct description of it. Nevertheless, in most cases the speaker's word counts as authoritative, and the statement is verified (or falsified) by the subject himself when he utters it. Statement (2b), on the other hand, can go wrong in more ways. The possibilities of error are multiplied in this case, but added to those already mentioned is the problem of consulting a sufficiently large number of persons concerning their experiences. Despite these complications, however, if the reports of others are accepted, (2b) is also verifiable in some degree. The most relevant difference between (2a) and (2b) is that the one can be established by the subject himself, whereas the reports of many persons must be relied upon to confirm the other. Pyrrho's position, as determined thus far, does not rule out either alternative.

Returning to the denial of truth and falsity, we may suppose that perceptual statements, which make a claim about the nature of something, would be included in that denial.[11] Sense statements, on the other hand, are acceptable, because they function merely as reports of experience. It would be incautious to conclude on this basis, however, that Pyrrho would have considered sense statements to be true or false. If the concept of truth is linked to a representative view of perception, it is un-

---

[11] The same seems to hold of ethical judgments. Timon (*Poet.*, frag. 70) says about them: ἀλλὰ πρὸς ἀνθρώπων ταῦτα νόῳ κέκριται. See also *Vit.*, IX, 61; Suidas (*Πύρρων*), *Lexicon* (Berlin, 1854).

likely that such an alternative would have occurred to
him. A perceptual statement makes a claim about the
properties of an object, which on that perceptual model
implies that experience is taken to be representative of
the object. When it is established that this condition is
fulfilled, the experience as well as the resulting belief
and, presumably, the perceptual statement are true, but
all are false when the condition is not fulfilled. In the
case of sense statements, however, the question whether
experience accurately represents the world does not
arise. For this reason, in spite of the acceptability of
sense statements, it is perhaps nonetheless inappropri-
ate, from the standpoint of the early Skeptics, to call
them true or false. The most important difference between a sense statement and a perceptual statement is
not that the one can be called true (or false), whereas
the other cannot, but that in uttering a sense statement
of either form (2a) or (2b), we are not at the same time
generating an epistemological problem of matching
experience with its object. This difference provides the
most plausible explanation of the Pyrrhonist's stance
with respect to each type of assertion.

It is noteworthy that the Pyrrhonists have a special
term to designate what is experienced by a percipient,
hence, what is actually reported by a sense statement.
The term "phenomenon" (φαινόμενον), a substantive from
"to appear" (φαίνεσθαι), means an "appearance" of something. The distinction between phenomenon and existing object is parallel to that between "appears" and
"is"; and epistemologically it marks a difference between the object as it is perceived and the object as it
exists in some other circumstance, probably one independent of its being experienced.[12] In the light of this

---

[12] The term φαινόμενον is not new in Greek philosophy with the
Skeptics, but it is consistently employed by Pyrrhonists with
the technical sense mentioned. Timon's use of φύειν (n. 3) suggests
that φαινόμενον was contrasted with φύσις by the early Pyrrhonists.
Besides φύσις a favorite term of later Pyrrhonists for "real object"
was ὑποκείμενον.

new term, then, we may suppose that the phenomenon is what is experienced, as contrasted with the autonomous object. Since the latter is held to be what exists (ἔστι, πέφυκε), while the former is what appears (φαίνεται), that is, what is apparent to us, it would seem to follow that the objects of our experience are the appearances of existents rather than the existent themselves.

Timon says with characteristic obscurity:

> But the phenomenon prevails on every side, wherever it may go.[13]

The fragment can be interpreted variously, depending on the implications of "prevails." Perhaps its most obvious meaning, in view of Pyrrho's denial that the nature of things is known along with his willingness to acknowledge their appearances, is that the phenomenon prevails over the perceiving subject, preventing him from apprehending the existent. Acting as a curtain between subject and object, it screens the real world from his view. Timon may also mean, however, that the phenomenon prevails by commanding acceptance. That is, though we do not claim that honey really is sweet, we do (cannot help but) grant that it appears (tastes) sweet.[14] Both these meanings are implicit in the passage, and the ambiguity is probably quite intentional.[15]

SKEPTIC STANDARD. Sextus Empiricus offers a similar explanation of the lines quoted above, when he suggests that Timon intends the phenomenon to be a standard or criterion (κριτήριον) for the conduct of life. Ignorance of the real character of things necessitates that our ac-

---

[13] *Poet.*, frag. 69: ἀλλὰ τὸ φαινόμενον πάντη σθένει, οὗπερ ἂν ἔλθῃ.

[14] This was later the view of Sextus Empiricus, who held that the acceptance of phenomena was thus necessitated psychologically. Cf. *PH*, I, 19, 22.

[15] The quotation is from Timon's Ἰνδαλμοί, in which there is probably a deliberate play on the title itself. It means both "appearances" and "illusions."

tions be guided by phenomena. Thus before citing the fragment Sextus remarks:

> It was necessary for the Skeptic, unless he was to be entirely inactive, taking no part in the affairs of daily life, to have some criterion of preference and aversion, that is, the phenomenon.[16]

This interpretation may be reinforced by the following passage from the same poem of Timon, the ambiguity of which is best preserved in literal translation.

> For I shall say (I question), as it appears to me to be,
> A word (myth) of truth, since I possess the right standard,
> That the nature of the divine and eternal good
> Enable man to live most equably.[17]

Commentary. The occurrence of "standard" (κανών) in the above lines is of interest, since it is one of the terms employed by Stoics and later Skeptics in their celebrated disputes over the "criterion" of truth.[18] On one reading ("I shall say a word of truth . . .") it looks as if Timon is claiming a standard of truth, which would contradict the view discussed earlier that beliefs about the nature of things are neither true nor false. Yet everything said is qualified by "as it appears to me to be," an indication that he is merely reporting his own experience. A plausible explanation is that Timon is equating what "appears" to be the case (phenomenon) with a standard, but not necessarily a criterion of truth.[19] The standard referred to may be a criterion

---

[16] *M*, VII, 30.

[17] *Poet.*, frag. 68:

ἦ γὰρ ἐγὼν ἐρέω, ὥς μοι καταφαίνεται εἶναι,
μῦθον ἀληθείης ὀρθὸν ἔχων κανόνα,
ὡς ἡ τοῦ θείου τε φύσις καὶ τἀγαθοῦ αἰεί,
ἐξ ὧν ἰσότατος γίνεται ἀνδρὶ βίος.

[18] *Vit.*, VII, 42; *M*, VII, 27; *M*, II, 80. It was also the title of a work by Democritus. Cf. *M*, VII, 138; VIII, 327.

[19] Later Pyrrhonists distinguished between a criterion of truth and a criterion for the conduct of life. The phenomenon was a

for living "most equably," that is, a criterion for the conduct of life. If this is the case, the "divine and eternal good" implies no more than the Pyrrhonic goal of ataraxia. On the other hand (reading "I question a myth of truth . . ."), if we again suppose that what "appears" is the standard referred to, the "myth" challenged may be the view that knowledge of the "nature" of things, specifically the "divine and eternal good" as suggested by traditional philosophers, is what leads to a most equable existence. This "truth" would be disputed by a Pyrrhonist, who realizes that the "nature" of things is unknowable and, accordingly, adopts the "right standard" (phenomenon).

SKEPTIC ATTITUDE

Let us turn now to Pyrrho's second question, which concerns the proper attitude to adopt toward those things whose character cannot be known.[20] Since our sense experiences and beliefs are neither true nor false, "therefore, we ought not to put our trust in them, but be without beliefs, disinclined to take a stand one way or the other, and steadfast in this attitude."[21]

Commentary. Pyrrho's answer is a recommendation that follows from his reply to the first question. He declares that we ought not to put our trust in beliefs and experiences that are neither true nor false, presumably meaning by this that we ought not to affirm or deny their truth. As he goes on to explain, this is in effect a prohibition against holding beliefs (ἀδόξαστοι),[22] — against taking a positive or negative stand (ἀκλινεῖς) with respect to matters that cannot be known. It is clear that Pyrrho's restriction is meant to apply to beliefs that would be

---

criterion in the second sense. Cf. *PH*, 1, 21–23; *M*, VII, 30; *Subfig.* (Deichgräber, *Die Griechische Empirikerschule*, p. 82).

[20] τίνα χρὴ τρόπον ἡμᾶς πρὸς αὐτὰ διακεῖσθαι;

[21] διὰ τοῦτο οὖν μηδὲ πιστεύειν αὐταῖς δεῖν, ἀλλ' ἀδοξάστους καὶ ἀκλινεῖς καὶ ἀκραδάντους εἶναι . . .

[22] Timon (*Poet.*, frag. 48) praises Pyrrho for having escaped the servitude of δόξα. See also frag. 72.

expressed as perceptual statements. For these (rather than sense statements) make claims that cannot be established in experience. He next introduces a correlative piece of advice — a formula for facilitating the agnosticism recommended concerning belief. If the question should arise whether or not something is the case, the Pyrrhonist, knowing that questions about the nature of things cannot be decided, should reply that it "no more is than is not, than both is and is not, than neither is nor is not."[23] This formula is not to be construed as an affirmation or denial of anything; it merely expresses the speaker's inability to accept either alternative presented. Signifying the refusal to make an assertion, it is a device to undermine argument by blocking discussion. Accordingly, Diogenes Laertius reports:

The utterance ("No more") therefore means, according to what Timon says in the *Python*, "the fact of determining nothing, but withholding assent."[24]

The locution in question is one of the first of the many slogans subsequently to be employed by Pyrrhonists with the same pragmatic purpose.[25] These sayings

---

[23] περὶ ἑνὸς ἑκάστου λέγοντας ὅτι οὐ μᾶλλον ἔστιν ἢ οὐκ ἔστιν, ἢ καὶ ἔστι καὶ οὐκ ἔστιν, ἢ οὔτε ἔστιν οὔτε οὐκ ἔστιν.

The clause may also be read: "saying about each thing individually that it no more is than is not, or that it both is and is not, or that it neither is nor is not." The formula was shortened by later Skeptics to, "No more this than that," and was usually cited in the even more abbreviated form, "No more" (οὐ μᾶλλον). The locution is not original with the Skeptics. Though employed somewhat differently, it is found in the writings of Plato, Aristotle, and others. See Phillip DeLacy, "οὐ μᾶλλον and the Antecedents of Ancient Skepticism,"*Phronesis*, 3 (1958), 59–71. The testimony of Theophrastus (*De Sens.*, 69, quoted in *Vor.*, II, 119, 18–19) and Sextus Empiricus (*PH*, I, 213) that Democritus and his followers used the expression in connection with the unreliability of sense perception is interesting in view of Pyrrho's alleged connection with the Democritean school.

[24] *Poet.*, frag. 80: . . . σημαίνει οὖν ἡ φωνή, καθά φησι Τίμων ἐν τῷ Πύθωνι, 'τὸ μηδὲν ὁρίζειν, ἀλλ' ἀπροσθετεῖν.' Cf. *Vit.*, IX, 76; *PH*, I 206–209.

[25] For others see *PH*, I, 187–210; *Vit.*, IX, 74–77, 103–104.

were interpreted variously as interrogative, autobiographical — revealing the speaker's uncommitted state of mind — and even as assertions that refuted themselves along with all other dubious statements.[26] Expressed as a question the "No more" formula can be translated "Why this more than that?" or, as Timon is said to have put it, "Why yes, why no, why the question 'why' itself?"[27] Invoking the Skeptic formula is thus an effective procedure for enabling the Pyrrhonist to free himself of doubtful beliefs, subverting fruitless discussion in the process.[28] Pyrrho's answer to the second question, in short, is to suspend judgment with respect to questions about the nature of things.

OUTCOME OF SKEPTICISM

Pyrrho's final concern is with the end result of the suspense of judgment proposed.[29] For those who assume the appropriate attitude, he says, "there will result, first, a disinclination to make assertions and, then, ataraxia."[30] Those following the favored program will acquire a natural disposition to remain neutral in regard to unanswerable questions. This state of mind (ἀφασία),[31] in which one is averse to making any assertions positive or negative, is followed by ataraxia, the Pyrrhonic con-

[26] For later interpretations of the Skeptic sayings see *Vit.*, IX, 74–77, 103–104; *PH*, I, 189–192, 197, 200–201, 203, 206.

[27] Aristocles in *Pr. Ev.*, XIV, 18, 759c (*Poet.*, p. 176).

[28] Another typical Skeptic procedure for remaining ἀδόξαστος but usually associated with later Skeptics, was to argue persuasively on both sides of a question. Some of the fragments of Timon (*Poet.*, frags. 45, 46, 59) indicate that the early Pyrrhonists may also have seen the usefulness of such a method. Timon praises Zeno the Eleatic for being ἀμφοτερόγλωσσος and Democritus for being ἀμφίνοος, whereas Xenophanes is gently censured for not being sufficiently ἀμφοτερόβλεπτος.

[29] τί περιέσται τοῖς οὕτως ἔχουσι;

[30] τοῖς μέντοι γε διακειμένοις οὕτω περιέσεσθαι Τίμων φησὶ πρῶτον μὲν ἀφασίαν, ἔπειτα δ' ἀταραξίαν.

[31] Sextus (*PH*, I, 192) explains: . . . ὡς εἶναι ἀφασίαν πάθος ἡμέτερον δι' ὃ οὔτε τιθέναι τι οὔτε ἀναιρεῖν φαμέν.

ception of well-being.[32] The outcome of the Skeptic's enlightenment, therefore, is an untroubled state of mental calm, marked by the absence of efforts to know the unknowable.

Commentary. The substance of Pyrrho's doctrine, insofar as we are able to judge from the extant fragments, seems to be as follows: The nature of things is beyond our grasp, with the result that none of our beliefs (or experiences) about these realities is either true or false. We ought therefore to suspend judgment (ἀπροσθετεῖν) with respect to questions that arise in this connection, since by doing so we achieve the kind of spiritual quietude that constitutes human well-being. It is appropriate to ask at this point exactly what Pyrrho is rejecting and what he is advocating.

The available fragments suggest that Pyrrho's Skepticism constitutes no more than a repudiation of philosophic speculation. It signifies an unwillingness to accept any theory about the nature of things. One theory is "no more" acceptable than another, because none is verifiable in experience. The evidence for this interpretation is, first of all, the wording of Pyrrho's initial question, which indicates that he is specifically addressing himself to theories about φύσις, philosophical theories that purport to disclose the real "nature" of things. Secondly, the fragments of Timon abound in criticism and ridicule of philosophers, both predecessors and contemporaries, who were the exponents of such theories.[33] And finally, the accounts of Pyrrho's life and opinions that have come down to us are in substantial agreement that Pyrrho himself was principally a moralist, who

---

[32] Cf. *Vit.*, IX, 107. Sextus (*PH*, I, 29) says: "And the Skeptics therefore were expecting to gain ataraxia by coming to a decision regarding the disparity of things phenomenal and conceptual, but being unable to do this, they suspended judgment. And supervening upon their suspense of judgment, as if by chance, was ataraxia, just as a shadow follows its object."

[33] See, for example, *Poet.*, frags. 28, 34, 35, 36, 38, 41, 42, 43, 51.

did not espouse "dogmatic" (speculative) doctrines.[34]
There is also reason to suppose, on the other hand, that
he advocated attending to the affairs of ordinary life. We
are told that he accepted phenomena as a basis for action and followed the dictates of custom and convention.[35] Moreover, Diogenes Laertius reports that Timon
claimed not to have "gone beyond ordinary custom"[36]
and takes him in the context of that remark to be referring to his own philosophical views. Pyrrho's skepticism
thus seems to amount to a renunciation of traditional
philosophical theories, which in his case apparently
meant a wholesale rejection of philosophy, and a return
to the practical affairs of life.

Still, there is something paradoxical about Pyrrho's
conclusion, which is intended to do away with philosophy, in the light of his initial advice to the seeker of
well-being to ponder the philosophical question of the
nature of things. The only course of action consistent
with the Skeptic position would seem to be to do something other than philosophy. This raises a question
about the relation between philosophy and ataraxia.
Pyrrho seems to hold that the two are incompatible
but that one is a means to the other. He is proposing,
in effect, that the seeker of well-being philosophize in
order to give up philosophy. It is apparent that the

---

[34] *Vit.*, IX, 106; *PH*, I, 7; *Ac.*, II, 130; *Fin.*, IV, 49; *Epiph.
Advers. Haeres.*, III, 18 (*Dox.*, p. 591). But see also *Vit.*, IX, 68.

[35] *Vit.*, IX, 61, 62, 106; Aristocles in *Pr. Ev.* XIV, 18, 762a (*Poet.*,
p. 179); cf. *PH*, I, 17.
Some of the anecdotes related by Diogenes Laertius (*Vit.*, IX,
62–63) seem to suggest otherwise; but these tales, which are
probably in part responsible for a popular tradition that represents Pyrrhonism as a philosophy cultivating insensibility and in-
difference toward everything, cannot be regarded as a reliable
basis for determining Pyrrho's philosophy.

[36] *Poet.*, frag. 81: καὶ ὁ Τίμων ἐν τῷ Πύθωνί φησι μὴ ἐκβεβηκέναι τὴν
συνήθειαν.
Other possible (if less likely) readings in the context are:
"Timon in the *Python*" (1) "denies that he has gone beyond the
ordinary usage of language," and (2) "denies that the ordinary
usage of language has been fulfilled."

Pyrrhonist's goal of well-being is not the traditional ideal of the speculative philosopher. Speculation as such is incompatible with an untroubled spirit. Nevertheless, the Pyrrhonist is released from the "servitude" of belief and opinion only by the realization that the object of his speculation cannot be known. By raising and answering the appropriate philosophical questions he becomes emancipated from philosophy. It is his liberation that is a necessary condition of well-being.

The moral context in which Pyrrho's Skepticism is contained is clearly an important part of his philosophical position. This practical orientation, though it remains throughout the Skeptic movement, becomes increasingly less intrinsic to the character of the later Skeptic philosophies as the issues surrounding Pyrrho's first philosophical question are discussed in detail and with greater sophistication. The epistemology of later Pyrrhonism emerges from the rudimentary ideas and distinctions embedded in Pyrrho's (essentially) moral philosophy, but it subsequently seems to stand on its own, having little apparent connection with the practical goal of well-being that is (at least nominally) at its foundation.

PYRRHONISM AND THE PHILOSOPHIC TRADITION

We have examined the fragments of the early Pyrrhonists in the hope of gaining a glimmer of insight into the origin of the Skeptic movement. It is also of interest in this connection to consider Pyrrho's philosophy in relation to the tradition from which it arises. In particular, we may ask in what respects, if any, it departs from that tradition and to what extent his view that reality cannot be known is a novel one among Greek philosophers.

Embedded in this position, as already noted, is a dualism between appearances and reality, which was a commonplace in Greek philosophy by the time of Pyrrho. The world has a twofold nature, the phenomenal and the real. We are acquainted with its phenomenal aspect through sense perception, which, however, is inadequate to disclose its real nature. So far the Skeptic position is quite orthodox. It originated within an intellectual context in which the appearance-reality dichotomy was so familiar as to be taken quite for granted. But the likeness seems to end here. Parmenides, Democritus, Plato, and others who drew the above distinction held the view that, even though inaccessible to sense, the real world can be known by the intellect. The senses, it is true, are capable of grasping no more than sensible objects, but mind is competent to grasp intelligibles. Reality for these philosophers is intelligble to mind. Its apprehension is what is meant by knowledge, as contrasted with belief whose object is the phenomenal. The Pyrrhonist, on the contrary, denies that the real nature of things can be discerned at all. This entails a disavowal of both sense perception and reason as sufficient to apprehend the real.

The Pyrrhonic distrust of sense perception is not surprising in view of the philosophic tradition mentioned. It may indeed have been supported by reasons or arguments that have not come down to us, or it may merely reflect an uncritical acceptance of a philosophic "truism" inherited from predecessors. A denial of the efficacy of reason, however, though not unprecedented among Greek philosophers, is nonetheless more noteworthy. There is no explicit statement of such a position in the extant fragments, but it is implicit in Pyrrho's declaration that things are by nature "indeterminable." [37] That assertion rules out all insights of reason along with

---

[37] There is one fragment that might be taken to contradict this. Timon (*Poet.*, frag. 44) praises Parmenides for having brought forth νώσεις instead of the deception of φαντασία. But the passage does not necessarily imply approval of Parmenides' philosophy or of the view that real can be apprehended by thought alone. The contrast may merely be between the "intelligence" of Parmenides (for having renounced the testimony of sense) and the fraudulent "imaginings" of others. See frag. 59 and *Vit.*, IX, 61.

beliefs (δόξαι), whose origin and object are the world of sense. It is tantamount to a denial that we apprehend anything other than appearances.

Our information about the early Pyrrhonists is too limited to contain an explanation for the dismissal of reason from its traditionally privileged position as knower of the real. Nevertheless, we can hazard a guess at explanation by looking for unstated but likely assumptions that would make the Pyrrhonist's view a reasonable one. One such possibility suggests itself. Pyrrho's doctrine is representative of both the traditional notion that the object of sense experience (and belief) is the phenomenal, whereas the object of knowledge is the real, and the assumption, not strictly a part of this tradition (though probably inherited from Aristotle), that knowledge has its origin in the data of sensory experience.[38] The introduction of this "empiricist axiom," which denies reason independent access to the real world, renders the Pyrrhonic philosophy not only plausible but a necessary consequence of certain premises. Sense experience reveals no more than the phenomenal character of the world, but to know is to apprehend the real. Yet knowledge must be a product of what is given in sensory experience, because the mind has no direct intuition of its own. Since there is nothing to bridge the gap between appearance and object, there is apparently no alternative to the Skeptic position. To know the real nature of things entails being able to establish that experience conforms to its object, but to be in a position to accomplish that requires knowledge of the object independent of sense experience, which the Skeptic's empiricism rules out.

Our study of the early Pyrrhonists ends with these speculations. To follow the course of the skeptical movement in Greek thought during this period, we must

---

[38] This empiricist doctrine was an important part of Stoic epistemology. Zeno of Citium, the founder of Stoicism, was a contemporary of both Pyrrho and Timon.

look next to Plato's Academy where the spirit of philosophical criticism found powerful expression. Though Academic Skepticism flourished during the period immediately following the first appearance of Pyrrhonism, logically it is not a development of Pyrrhonism but a second, and rather different, skeptical philosophy.

3 * ACADEMIC SKEPTICISM

The contribution made by Academic Skeptics toward a clearer understanding of epistemological problems current among Hellenistic philosophers is the outcome of a lively controversy with the Stoics over the problem of the criterion of truth. Insofar as their doctrine consists of an attack on the Stoic theory of knowledge, it is entirely "skeptical" in the modern sense of the term, destructive in intent and negative in conclusion. The other side of the Academic philosophy, however, issues in more positive results. A direct product of the attack on Stoicism, it attempts to offer a solution to the problems of knowledge exposed and hence brought into sharper focus by that very process of criticism. This chapter treats the two aspects of the Academic philosophy separately, first the polemic against Stoicism and then the effort to deal effectively with issues clarified by that criticism.

As a preface to the study of Skepticism in the Academy it is necessary to begin with a brief account of the Stoic theory of knowledge.[1]

STOIC DOCTRINE OF IMPRESSIONS

The Stoic account of knowledge rests on an empiricist psychology that provides an explanation of the genesis of knowledge from its simplest raw materials. All knowledge has its origin in experience. Thus the Stoics main-

---

[1] The compressed summary of Stoic theory that follows is not meant to be complete, but includes only those features relevant to the Skeptic critique. Unless mention is made to the contrary, the Stoic doctrines are treated as a body. A fuller account can be found in E. V. Arnold, *Roman Stoicism* (Cambridge, 1911).

tained that the mind at birth is a blank sheet of paper on which data (termed "impressions") are inscribed from an external source.[2] The notion of impression (φαντασία)[3] is of major importance in the Stoic theory. It is central to their account of the origin of knowledge and is, accordingly, the most important component in the resulting definition.

PSYCHOLOGY. Stoic philosophers divided the contents of the mind into impressions and concepts formed from them.[4] They went on to define an impression literally as an "imprint (τύπωσις) on the mind (ἡγεμονικόν)," analogous to that made by a seal on wax.[5] Transmitted via sense organs, it is ordinarily occasioned by the presence of a perceptual object, as in veridical and distorted perception, but less commonly is no more than an empty phantasm (φάντασμα), for example, hallucinations and dream images. Nevertheless, the impression is in most cases a copy, whether perfect or imperfect, of its original and is a necessary condition of our apprehending that object.[6] By rearranging impressions and the memories of impressions in various ways (compounding, transposing, enlarging), we form abstract notions that allow us to deal conceptually with the objects perceived by sense.[7]

[2] Aetius, *Placita*, IV, 11 (SVF, II, 28, 13); cf. *Vit.*, VII, 49; *M*, VIII, 356.

[3] The term φαντασία occurs once in the extant fragments of Timon (*Poet.*, frag. 44), but it appears neither to have a technical sense in that fragment nor to play any role in the Pyrrhonist epistemology. As used by Timon, it probably means no more than "imagination."

[4] Aetius, *op. cit.*; *Vit.*, VII, 52–53; *M*, VIII, 58; IX, 393–396; *Ac.*, II, 30.

[5] This definition was put forward by early Stoics, but owing to objections brought against it, it was later refined by Chrysippus to read "alteration (ἑτεροίωσις, ἀλλοίωσις) of the mind." See *Vit.*, VII, 45–46, 50; *PH*, II, 70; *M*, VII, 228–231, 372–377; VIII, 400.

[6] *Vit.*, VII, 51–54; *M*, VII, 242–250; VIII, 67; Aetius, *op. cit.*

[7] The Stoics maintained that, in addition to impressions of sense (αἰσθητικαὶ φαντασίαι), there were also rational impressions

Proceeding from that analysis, the Stoics were in a position to define knowledge as the unerring apprehension (κατάληψις) of a real entity through the intermediary impression.[8] In the case of knowledge of the material world three conditions are necessary: an impression must be produced in the percipient; the impression must be true; the percipient must give firm assent (συγκατάθεσις) to the impression. Weak assent and assent to a false impression result in belief and error respectively. Zeno the Stoic illustrated this conception of knowledge with a metaphor, likening impressions to an open hand with fingers outstretched, assent to the hand with fingers partially contracted, apprehension to the hand closed tightly forming a fist, and knowledge to the closed fist grasped firmly by the other hand.[9]

CRITERION OF TRUTH. It is clear from the preceding definition of knowledge that the true impression plays a

---

(λογικαὶ φαντασίαι). (*Vit.*, VII, 51, 63; *M*, VIII, 70, 85–87, 409–410). These entities are a source of difficulty, since they were also referred to as "thoughts" and "concepts." But unlike the concepts mentioned above, they did not originate in sense experience. They were analogous to sense impressions, being occasioned by real, though incorporeal (hence imperceptible), entities, which the Stoics called "lekta." A lekton (λεκτόν) is what is *meant*, when we say something, and is to be distinguished from the object talked about. Propositions (ἀξιώματα) are included among these incorporeal lekta. See Benson Mates, *Stoic Logic*, chap. ii (2d print.; Berkeley and Los Angeles, 1961). Just as material objects are apprehended mediately through sense impressions, so too these incorporeal entities are grasped mediately through rational impressions. We have impressions, for example, of propositions and of logical sequence (called "transitive" or "compound" impressions). (*M*, VII, 416–421; VIII, 271, 276, 288, 409–410; *Vit.*, VII, 52, 53.) The obscurities of the rational impression seem to be related to similar difficulties connected with the lekton. Sextus (*M*, VIII, 70, 85–87) complains that the lekton is defined by reference to the rational impression, and the latter by reference to the former. The lekton is a major exception to an otherwise materialist ontology and, along with the rational impression, to a theory of knowledge placing the origin of knowledge in sense experience.

[8] *M*, VII, 151; *Vit.*, VII, 47; *Ac.*, I, 41.

[9] *Ac.*, I, 40–41; II, 145.

crucial role in Stoic doctrine. Their account shifts at this point from a psychological inquiry into the origin of knowledge to a concern with epistemological problems that emerge in connection with the theory. For the question immediately arises: "How are true impressions to be distinguished from false ones?" It was necessary for the Stoics to formulate a criterion of truth which would make it possible systematically to distinguish between true and false impressions.

They began by defining a true (false) impression as one that is expressible as a true (false) proposition. My impression that it is light is true, if the proposition "It is light" is true; if not, the impression is false.[10] They were then obliged to explain the conditions under which a proposition is true, which they accomplished by reference to the facts or objects mentioned in it. The proposition "It is light" is true if, and only if, it is in fact light.[11] But the last move merely shifts the problem to another level. How do we know what the facts are? The Stoics seem to have responded to that question by looking again to the impression. In an apparent effort to avoid circularity they invoked a special kind of impression as the criterion of truth (κριτήριον ἀληθείας). A "cataleptic" (καταληπτική) impression is one that literally "grasps" its object, resulting necessarily in knowledge of the object.[12] Such an impression cannot be doubted. It carries its own guarantee of truth along with it, since

[10] I use "proposition" instead of "statement" only with reference to the Stoic doctrine. Truth and falsity (according to the Stoics) were properties chiefly of propositions, and every proposition was true or false (*Vit.*, VII, 65, 66; *M*, VII, 243–244, VIII, 10–12, 70). A proposition (ἀξίωμα) was an intelligible, incorporeal entity, which could be either immediately evident (πρόδηλον, ἐναργές) or nonevident (ἄδηλον). The immediately evident was defined as whatever is present to sense or mind, requiring no further evidence to establish it, such as at the present moment that it is day and the corresponding perceptual proposition. The nonevident is anything that, for one reason or another, is not immediately evident, such as whether the stars are even or odd in number. Cf. *PH*, II, 97; *M*, VII, 364; VIII, 141, 316.

[11] *Vit.*, VII, 65; *M*, VIII, 100.

[12] Since I know of no English term that reproduces the technical

it is (1) caused by an existing object, (2) an exact replica of that entity, and (3) of such a nature that it could have no other origin.[13] A cataleptic impression is so striking and clear as to compel assent.

> For [the cataleptic impression] by its clarity and force all but grasps us by the hair, as they say, and drags us down to assent, standing in need of nothing else for its impact or for suggesting its superiority over the others.[14]

Commentary. One effect of the Stoic criterion of truth is a redefinition of knowledge in terms of the cataleptic impression. Since knowledge is firm assent to a cataleptic impression, questions of epistemological interest can be expected to cluster around that notion. It is of particular importance, therefore, to see more clearly how the cataleptic impression functions in the Stoic theory. Let us consider its stated characteristics. The first two features specify the necessary and sufficient conditions of truth, whereas the third is meant to distinguish the cataleptic impression from other true impressions. It is (experienced as) of such a nature as to have originated necessarily in that object of which it is in fact the exact replica. It is difficult to know what the Stoics meant by this beyond the fact that our assent to such an impression is necessitated or compelled in a manner not characteristic of other experience. Yet we may wonder what is involved in giving assent to an impression and also how assent to a cataleptic impression differs from assent to any other true impression. It

---

meaning of the Stoic καταληπτικὴ φαντασία, I shall retain the above transliterated version throughout the discussion that follows. The verb καταλαμβάνειν means "to lay hold of" or "to grasp." The Stoic criterion was subsequently modified, probably because of Academic criticism, to "catalepetic impression, provided that it has no obstacle," (that is, provided there is no reason for not accepting it). *M*, VII, 253 ff.

[13] *M*, VII, 248, 253–258, 402; *Vit.*, VII, 46–50; *Ac.*, II, 18, 33–34, 38. The circularity is obvious, since the cataleptic impression is defined by reference to the very facts whose existence it is alleged to confirm. See *M*, VII, 426.

[14] *M*, VII, 257.

would seem that to assent to an impression is, in effect, to assent to the proposition expressing its content.[15] That is, in assenting to the impression that it is light, I am implicitly giving my assent to the perceptual proposition "It is light," though I need not do so explicitly. Now if I assent (as I must, according to the Stoics) to a cataleptic impression that it is light, in this case too I am assenting to the corresponding proposition "It is light," but with the exception, presumably, that the proposition itself is also certain and indubitable, which was of course not true in the former case. Still, this does not explain the most important respect in which assent to a cataleptic impression differs from assent to other true impressions. That difference can be brought out only by observing that the special mark of certainty which intrinsically characterizes cataleptic impressions *authorizes* assent by the same fact that it *compels* assent. That is, a cataleptic impression "generates"[16] a proposition that is immediately evident and certain, requiring no supporting evidence beyond the unquestionable experience of the subject himself. The role of the cataleptic impression is therefore apparent. In addition to defining the conditions of truth, it authorizes a claim to knowledge. And, on the Stoic account, this means it insures that the conditions of truth are satisfied.

ACADEMIC CRITICISM

Academic criticism of the Stoic criterion was perforce an attack on the notion of a cataleptic impression.[17]

---

[15] Arcesilaus quibbled on this score that assent is given, not to impressions, but to propositions (*M*, VII, 154).

[16] The exact relation of a perceptual proposition to its corresponding sense impression is obscure. If impressions are caused by real entities, and if, accordingly, certain (rational) impressions are occasioned by propositions or lekta (*M*, VIII, 85–87), what is the relation between a sense impression, which is caused by a physical object, and the corresponding perceptual proposition? Cf. *Ac.*, II, 21.

[17] Unless specific mention is made of Arcesilaus, the critique

But the Academics made no effort to repudiate the psychology at the base of the doctrine. In fact, they accepted the theory of impressions as such and the perceptual model that it suggests. When the sense organ is affected by contact with one of the clear and evident objects in its range, we perceive that object.[18] Since perception cannot occur without sensory affection, the (Stoic) impression must be an affection ($\pi\acute{a}\theta os$) of the perceiving subject representative both of itself and of the object causing it.[19] They acknowledged accordingly that a criterion of truth, if there is such a thing, must be sought in sense impressions, for without them we would have no experience and, further, whatever is judged by reason is derived ultimately from impressions of sense.[20] But since not all impressions are true, they

of Stoic doctrine in this section represents the position of Carneades, which has survived in more detail.

[18] *M*, VII, 159–166. Sextus' account of the Academic position at 160–163 presents terminological problems. He uses his own term "phenomenon" ($\phi a\iota\nu\acute{o}\mu\epsilon\nu o\nu$) to designate the object that causes an impression (161). This term is characteristic of Pyrrhonic Skepticism, but there is no substantial evidence that the Academics used it. The passage mentioned is contradicted by Sextus' assertion at 167 that the impression is occasioned by the external object ($\dot{\epsilon}\kappa\tau\grave{o}s$ $\dot{v}\pi o\kappa\epsilon\acute{\iota}\mu\epsilon\nu o\nu$). See also 160 and 170. Sextus' introduction of "phenomenon" into his account of Carneades' epistemology may be just carelessness.

[19] *Ibid.*, 162. It is not clear what is meant by an impression's being "representative ($\pi a\rho a\sigma\tau a\tau\iota\kappa\acute{o}\nu$, $\dot{\epsilon}\nu\delta\epsilon\iota\kappa\tau\iota\kappa\acute{o}\nu$) of itself." That it should represent (or reveal) itself in the same way as it represents the object is implausible. In his exposition Sextus follows this statement with an example (apparently attributed to one of Carneades' successors as head of the Academy, Antiochus of Ascalon, who endorsed the Stoic doctrine), comparing impressions to light, which reveals both itself and the objects within it. An impression, then, (like light) makes perception of the object possible. The inference may also be intended that in perceiving an object, we are aware of perceiving it (being affected by it).

[20] *Ibid.*, 160–161, 165. The last part of the argument seems to be that since reason has no direct access, i.e., independent of sensory experience, to the truth, it cannot be the criterion. The reasoning may be dubious, but it provides a good statement of Academic empiricism.

cannot without qualification be accepted as the criterion. Many are not exact likenesses of their originals.
In cases of perceptual error an impression either mis-
represents its object or is excited by factors not indicated by its content.

> But since [the impression] does not always indicate truly
> the object that caused it, but often deceives and, like bad
> messengers, misrepresents those who dispatched it, there
> follows of necessity the impossibility of allowing every
> impression as a criterion of truth, but only, if any, the true
> one.[21]

It is clear that up to this point there is no substantial
difference between Stoic and Academic on the question
of perception. But in settling on the cataleptic impression as the criterion of truth, the Stoics were committed
to the view that these impressions carried with them a
distinctive mark of truth, setting them off from all
others and guaranteeing veridical perception. Both
Arcesilaus and Carneades repudiated that notion and,
consequently, the cataleptic impression.[22]

ARGUMENT AGAINST THE STOIC CRITERION. Carneades advanced the following argument against the Stoic
theory: [23]

   1. Some impressions are true and others false.
   2. A false impression is not cataleptic.
   3. If two impressions are indistinguishable, it is impossible for one to be cataleptic and the other not.
   4. For every true impression it is possible for a false
impression to be indistinguishable from it.
   5. Therefore, there is no cataleptic impression.

---

[21] *Ibid.*, 163; cf. *Ac.*, II, 47–48.
[22] *M*, VII, 155, 402; *Ac.*, I, 41, 45; II, 77–78, 103, 119, 148;
Pr. Ev., XIV, 4, 726d; 8, 736d.
[23] *Ac.*, II, 40–43, 47–50, 83 ff.; cf. *M*, VII, 163–166; 403 ff. What
follows is Carneades' principal argument. Other less important
arguments can also be found in the passages cited.

The fourth premise constitutes a major challenge to the Stoics, since the cataleptic impression was said to be of such a nature that a false impression could *not* be like it.[24] Premise 4 asserts, however, that there is *no* true impression such that a false one cannot be experienced that is indistinguishable from it. And if so, the truth of all impressions, no matter how striking and clear, can be questioned.

To support their contention that no recognizable sign attaches to certain impressions establishing their truth, the Skeptics noted that we often assent to false impressions and act accordingly. That is, we erroneously take such experience to be true, a clear sign both of the power of the experience to compel assent and of our ignorance in respect of the error. The fact of error confirms that the false impressions experienced on such occasions are indistinguishable from true ones. In line with this reasoning Academics produced a large number of examples illustrating different types of perceptual error, which can be classified roughly as follows: [25]

1. Hallucinations. Heracles, in a state of madness, slew his own children by mistake, taking them to be the offspring of his enemy Eurystheus.

---

[24] The Stoics apparently held also that some rational impressions were cataleptic. Characterized by the same mark of truth as cataleptic sense impressions, they guaranteed the existence and truth of the corresponding propositions (*M*, VII, 416–421; *M*, VIII, 70, 85–87).

[25] For the examples that follow and others see *M*, VII, 402 ff. and *Ac.*, II, 79–96. Other examples, apparently pertaining to rational impressions, depend on certain linguistic and logical puzzles. For instance, if a cataleptic impression guarantees the truth of "Three is few," what about the propositions, "Ten is few," "Fifty is few," and "Fifty-one is few"? At what point does the impression cease to be cataleptic? Another example is afforded by the Liar Paradox. Is the proposition "If you say that you are lying and speak the truth, then you are lying" accompanied by a cataleptic impression or not? *M*, VII, 416–422; *Ac.*, II, 96. These examples and other comments concerning the formal character of deductive reasoning indicate that the Academics had little use for Stoic logic. Cf. *Ac.*, II, 91–99.

2. Dreams. A man in sleep who shouts out in terror is apparently quite unaware of any difference between the impressions of his dreams and those of waking life.

3. Illusions. A painting creates the illusion of depth and texture. The land, when observed by a person on board ship, appears to be moving. An oar immersed in water looks bent.

4. Limited sensory powers (range and discrimination). Objects disappear from sight at a distance. We are unable to identify objects at a distance. We cannot judge accurately the size of the sun by merely gazing at it in the sky. Identical twins are commonly mistaken for each other. Even the Stoic sage cannot distinguish between two eggs presented to him or between a hundred seals imprinted on a hundred pieces of wax by the same ring.

The above examples and other similar ones were intended to constitute a conclusive refutation of the Stoic criterion of truth. If false impressions can be as convincing as true ones, thereby causing misguided actions and mistaken perceptual judgments, this seems a sufficient reason for denying that they are intrinsically distinguishable from true ones. The Stoic doctrine embodies the notion of a qualitative difference between true and false impressions, experienced as such by the percipient, which the very existence of perceptual error repudiates. No true impression carries along with it a special recognizable mark of certainty, a "cataleptic" label, that serves to set it apart from all other experience. In short, there is no true impression such that it is impossible for a false one to be indistinguishable from it, which is to say, there is no cataleptic impression.

STOIC REPLY. Defenders of the Stoic doctrine were not persuaded by the Academic criticism.[26] A consequence

[26] The following defense of Stoicism probably represents the position of Antiochus of Ascalon, who as head of the Academy in the first century B.C., rejected Carneades' criticism and defended the Stoic view. *Ac.*, II, 51–59. See also *Ac.*, II, 43–45 for some sophistical objections to the Academic critique.

of the Skeptic argument, they reasoned, is that all experience is dubious, but the examples of perceptual "error" cited do not establish that conclusion. Some are cases of abnormal or deranged perception; others are illusions that would be likely to take in only the most unsophisticated; and the rest can be attributed to undue carelessness. We are liable to error, to be sure, when drunk, deranged, or careless, but that is no reason for concluding that we always are (or may be) mistaken. The experience of lunatics, drunkards, and dreamers casts no doubt whatever on the authoritative experiences of ordinary life. No one denies that some impressions are false or doubtful; in fact, many of the examples cited by the Academics illustrate just the sort of impression that the Stoic would *not* call cataleptic. And of course if assent is given to a questionable impression, the result may well be error. The wise man will merely withhold assent in such dubious cases.

The Stoics went on to examine some of the Academic examples in more detail. Dream experiences present no problem, they argued, for upon awaking no one judges his dreams to be on a par with his waking experience, whereas in sleep his critical powers do not function at full capacity. Similarly, in the case of insane persons,

> . . . at the beginning of their attack they are conscious that they are mad, and say that something is appearing to them that is not real; and also when the attack is subsiding they are conscious of it, and say things like the words of Alcmaeon: "But my mind agrees in no way with the vision of my eyes." [27]

Also, consider the case of normal persons, who know, even when daydreaming that their fantasies are not real and that their drunken feelings and perceptions are not to be trusted. It is absurd to suppose that such impressions are indistinguishable from true ones, when even

[27] *Ac.*, II, 52 (translated by H. Rackham).

the persons experiencing them are aware of their incongruities.

The Stoic response to the case of resembling impressions was equally straightforward. Of course similarities exist between things of the same sort, be they identical twins, eggs, or impressions made by the same ring. But that causes no difficulty for the theory. The wise man, confronted with two objects that he is unable to distinguish, will simply reserve judgment until he is able to make finer discriminations of the sort required. And here the Stoics noted that though two objects may not be distinguishable by a given percipient, it does not follow that they are intrinsically indistinguishable. That is, some persons have more acute powers of sensory discrimination than others. Abilities of this sort naturally vary with experience and practice, so that a casual acquaintance may address a child by the name of his twin, whereas his mother has no trouble telling her twins apart. A painter discerns colors and a musician tones that are not apparent to the ordinary person.

The Stoics concluded that Academic criticism failed to undermine the cataleptic impression as the criterion of truth. The examples of perceptual error merely emphasize the dubiousness of some impressions, which are of course not cataleptic as the Stoics agreed, but they do not show that all experience is questionable. The Skeptic position rests on the mistaken view that a few isolated errors of perception can call into question the veracity of all experience.

Commentary. The above rejoinder indicates that the Stoics took the Academic criticism of their position to be misguided, on the ground that examples of abnormal or bizarre perceptual experience have little to do with a doctrine that is specifically concerned with normal or ordinary experience. Their appeal to standard perceptual conditions in the case of cataleptic impressions makes this quite clear. Had they not mistaken the force of the Skeptic argument, their reasons for rejecting it might have been sound.

The Stoics are certainly right in insisting that the occurrence of abnormal perceptual experience does not as such impugn the reliability of all the testimony of sense. To suppose that it does is to lapse into the inconsistency of counting as evidence only those data that confirm errors in perception and rejecting all the rest as inadmissible. If sense is competent to disclose perceptual error, it must also be capable of confirming at least some experience as true. This holds even on the supposition that all perception is illusory. For, assuming that to be the case, one would no longer be in a position to discern *any* perceptual error by sense. To be sure, incongruities could be noted by comparison with "standard" perceptual experiences, but they would be of no help in uncovering the "universal" error of perception without the aid of a criterion independent of sensory experience. If sense perception as such is unreliable, *it* gives us no more right to speak of false impressions than of true. Consequently, examples of unusual perceptual experiences do not support the thesis that all experience is (or might be) illusory. And if that were the point of the Skeptic attack, it would be a failure

The Stoic reply, however, misses the point of the Academic criticism, which is not a generalized argument dealing with sense perception but a polemic against the cataleptic impression as a criterion of truth. The cataleptic impression was said to be (1) true (an exact replica of the object that causes it) and (2) of such a nature that it could have no other origin (its own guarantee of truth). The force of the Skeptic criticism seems to be that, first, given the conditions that define the truth of an impression, no impression can guarantee its own truth, and, second, the Stoic criterion is inadequate to distinguish between true and false impressions.

The important step in the Skeptic argument is the premise asserting that for any true impression it is possible for a false one to be indistinguishable from it. That premise challenges the notion that an impression can be its own certification, once the conditions defining a true impression are accepted. To say that a cataleptic impression is experienced as such as to have originated in the object of which it is an exact copy is to suggest that the cataleptic impression is experienced as different from any other impression. But that distinguishing feature seems to come to no more than the force and clarity of the experience and its ability to compel assent. Consequently, the Skeptic examples of perceptual error are most relevant here. If the only mark of certainty characterizing cataleptic impressions is sufficient force and clarity to compel assent, then any false impression at one time or another may be indubitable to someone, and by the same token many true impressions very likely will be questioned. The condition of the percipient — illness, drunkenness, insanity — is quite aside from the point at issue. The sole relevant consideration is that the experience be forceful enough to compel assent, and to this end any case of genuine error is sufficient. Such cases do not, as we have seen, establish that all perceptual experience is doubtful, but they do establish that not all clear and forceful impressions are true and, therefore, that clarity and force cannot either guarantee the truth of any single impression or distinguish it from false and doubtful ones. It is worth noting that the Academics concentrated their attack on the Stoic notion that a *single* impression can insure its own truth. Hence, though true, it is of no avail to point out (as the Stoics did) that a person on awaking discounts his dream experiences as unreal or that insane persons on occasion are aware that they are hallucinating. If such impressions are strong enough at the time they are experienced to compel assent, the Skeptic has made his point, namely, that they are not intrinsically distinguishable from true impressions.

> As if anybody would deny that a man that has woken up thinks that he has been dreaming, or that one whose madness has subsided thinks that the things that he saw during his madness were not true. But that is not the point at

issue; what we are asking is what these things looked like at the time when they were seen.[28]

The Skeptic criticism rests heavily on the claim that there is no recognizable feature characteristically belonging to true impressions considered individually that may not also belong to false impressions. The fact of perceptual error appears to support that claim. But what follows from the point made? The first consequence of course is that no impression can establish its own truth. Force and clarity quite obviously are not enough. But in view of the conditions that define true impressions, it is reasonable to ask what would be sufficient. The procedure actually implied by the Stoic criterion for guaranteeing the truth of impressions is the altogether impossible one of matching an impression against the object it is said to copy. The substance of the Academic criticism might therefore to put as follows: We cannot be certain that an impression is an exact copy of its object, since it is impossible to compare impressions with the objects they are alleged to resemble. In fact, that is exactly the point of the contention that true impressions are not intrinsically distinguishable from false ones. The cataleptic impression provides no way out of this difficulty. It cannot guarantee that the conditions of truth are satisfied. The result is that if we do perceive objects, we cannot be sure when we do (accurately) and when not.

Granted that the Academic criticism demonstrates the inadequacy of the Stoic criterion as a guarantee of true experience, it also results in a more serious consequence for the theory. The cataleptic impression is not adequate even to distinguish between true and false impressions and hence to settle disagreements of fact. The alleged mark of certainty again will not do, since false impressions can be as clear and forceful as true ones. But once the notion of such a distinguishing fea-

[28] *Ibid.*, 88 (Rackham).

ture is repudiated, the Stoics are left with no systematic way of discriminating true from false impressions.

> . . . for when that proper canon of recognition has been removed, even if the man himself whom you see is the man he appears to you to be, nevertheless you will not make that judgment, as you say it ought to be made, by means of a mark of such a sort that a false likeness could not have the same character.[29]

On the other hand, should the Stoics take refuge in their definition of the cataleptic impression as one about which it is (logically) impossible to be mistaken, they have still to provide a way of distinguishing a cataleptic impression from other impressions.

The above consequence seems to be fatal to the Stoic theory. It very likely prompted the misdirected remark that the Academic criticism renders everything uncertain.[30] The half-truth embedded in that comment points to the failure of the cataleptic impressions as a criterion of truth. For unless the Stoic criterion is abandoned, the Skeptic arguments have just that effect.

CARNEADES' SOLUTION TO THE SKEPTICAL PROBLEM

After disposing of the Stoic criterion, the Academics were obliged, according to Sextus Empiricus, to devise an alternative criterion for the "conduct of life" and the "attainment of happiness."[31] Apparently not satisfied with the Pyrrhonic solution, which recommended merely following the dictates of social convention without commitment or belief, they required some standard as a guide to action. Carneades' answer to that practical question was to submit a new criterion of truth.[32]

---

[29] *Ibid.*, 84 (Rackham).
[30] See, for example, *Ibid.*, 27, 54.
[31] *M*, VII, 158, 166; *PH*, I, 231.
[32] Although the criterion provides a basis for action, it is not limited to that. As a criterion of *truth* it also pertains to beliefs

THE PROBLEM. The attack on Stoicism ended with the conclusion that no impression is absolutely certain (cataleptic). Hence no impression can establish conclusively the truth of a perceptual proposition (statement). Carneades was evidently concerned to draw out the implications of that conclusion. If no impression guarantees its own truth, does it follow that all are false or dubious? If no perceptual statement is established by a cataleptic impression, are all such assertions unjustified? His contention that the class of things that are not certain (cataleptic) is not coincident with the class of things nonevident[33] seems to have been an answer to questions of this sort. A great many things are neither absolutely certain nor nonevident.[34] Although no perceptual statement as such is unquestionable, some merit our acceptance more than others.[35] Carneades apparently conceived the task of a criterion of truth to be that of deciding which perceptual statements are justifiable, even if none is immune from error.

ANALYSIS OF IMPRESSIONS. Carneades began his own search for a criterion by expanding the analysis of the concept of impression.[36] An impression is *of* something — more exactly, of two things. It is spoken of in reference to both its origin or cause (perceptual object) and its subject (percipient).[37] There are accordingly two relations

and assertions independently of their function in motivating action. Cf. *M*, VII, 175, 179. The criterion proposed by Arcesilaus, viz., the "reasonable" (τὸ εὔλογον), however, may have amounted to no more than a standard for action. Cf. *PH*, I, 232; *M*, VII, 158.

[33] *Pr. Ev.*, XIV, 7, 736d: διαφορὰν δὲ εἶναι ἀδήλου καὶ ἀκαταλήπτου, καὶ πάντα μὲν εἶναι ἀκατάληπτα, οὐ πάντα δὲ ἄδηλα. Cf. *Ac.*, II, 32, 34, 54.

[34] Sextus (*M*, VII, 106, 161) uses the term "evident" (ἐναργές), i.e., "within the range of perception," to designate the type of perceptual object that gives rise to impressions and statements of this class. These statements, therefore, can be described as evident but not absolutely certain. Objects outside the range of perception are nonevident (ἄδηλον).

[35] *Ac.*, II, 99, 111.

[36] *M*, VII, 167–169.

[37] Objective and subjective genitives in the Greek.

to be considered, namely, the impression as related to object and subject. With respect to the first, an impression is true when it conforms to the perceptual object and false when it does not so conform. The relation between impression and percipient, on the other hand, determines what is apparently true to the subject (ἡ φαινομένη ἀληθὴς φαντασία). Carneades looked for the criterion of truth in the second relation rather than the first.

He went on to examine the impression-subject relation more carefully.[38] Some impressions appear true and others not, which is merely to say that some are more convincing than others. He therefore termed the apparently true impression a "credible" (πιθανή) impression.[39] It is naturally convincing in contrast with those we are immediately inclined to question (ἀπίθανος). Any impression that is initially implausible, despite the fact that it might be true, is a poor risk for a criterion of truth. Eliminating that class of impressions, then, Carneades proceeded to sort out credible impressions into different groups. Not all are equally convincing; nor are they convincing for the same reasons. Some impressions, though no one would deny their credibility, are faint, indistinct, or unclear owing to less than optimum perceptual conditions, and they too are unacceptable as a criterion of truth. This leaves only that range of experience that is most apparent (evident, manifest) as an appropriate area in which to locate the criterion of truth. Carneades therefore settled on the credible impression as the criterion of truth, meaning by this (according to the foregoing qualifications) our most evident experience.

Commentary. The consequences of Carneades' analysis up to this point are worth noting. By calling

---

[38] *M*, VII, 169 ff.

[39] The apparently true (or credible) impression was also called ἔμφασις (*M*, VII, 169). This term suggests that an impression reflects its object. We see the object *in* the impression, just as we see something *in* a mirror.

attention to two relations relevant to the study of impressions and by distinguishing between them as he did, Carneades, in effect, drew a distinction between *conditions* and *criterion* of truth. Like the Stoics, he located the conditions under which an impression is true in its relation to an object, but he did not follow them in merging those same conditions with the criterion of truth. This divergence embodies Carneades' diagnosis of the failure of the Stoic theory and serves to underscore the point of his criticism. The Stoic requirement that the criterion be met only by guaranteeing the conditions of truth (as defined) is an impossibility. The resulting distinction is of considerable interest for its effect in clarifying and reshaping the epistemological problem of the criterion that plagued the Stoics, in such a way as to make it amenable to solution. The criterion of truth coincides with the apparently true, whereas the conditions of truth hold independently of what appears to be true. It follows, therefore, that to ask "What is the criterion of truth?" is not to inquire when a statement (belief, impression) is true, but to inquire "When are we justified in making an assertion (holding a belief, assenting to an impression)?" And Carneades' response to that question would be, "When the assertion (belief) is supported by our most credible experience." Nevertheless, it is also clear that though the criterion tells us what counts as acceptable ground for an assertion, it cannot guarantee that the assertion is true. That is, it allows the uncomfortable possibility that a statement may justifiably be made, even though it is in fact false.[40]

No Single Criterion of Truth. Although Carneades' analysis of impressions has effectively narrowed the

---

[40] Hence the Stoics complained (*Ac.*, II, 36): "What language moreover could be more absurd than their formula, 'It is true that this is a token or a proof of yonder object, and therefore I follow it, but it is possible that the object that it indicates may be either false or entirely non-existent'?" (Translated by H. Rackham).

problem of the criterion to one of justifying perceptual statements (beliefs), he apparently thought that the question, "What is the criterion?" was still too broad.[41] As a general question it admits of a general answer (κοινὸν κριτήριον), namely, "credible impressions," but this answer will not be sufficient in every set of circumstances to justify belief. Rather than a single criterion there will be criteria of truth that vary in an indeterminate manner along with the many circumstances of ordinary life.

> . . . just as in different matters they (the Academics) make use of a different impression, as they say, so too in different circumstances they do not follow the same impression.[42]

For instance, the importance of the matter in question plays a large part in determining what counts as good reason for a perceptual assertion. In ordinary matters of little consequence a clear and evident impression does permit such an assertion. For example, a man's impression that snow is white warrants the corresponding belief or statement that snow is white.[43] But statements of greater import require stronger support, according to Carneades, and in matters "pertaining to happiness" still more is needed. In short, the criterion fluctuates according to the significance of the perceptual statement in our lives.

> . . . just as in ordinary life, when we are investigating a small matter, we question one witness, but in a greater matter we examine several, and when the matter under investigation is of still greater importance, we cross-examine each of the witnesses from the testimony of the others.[44]

[41] *M*, VII, 173: "And, being the criterion, it has considerable range . . . ."

[42] *Ibid.*, 185. The exposition that follows is based on *Ibid.*, 184–190; *PH*, I, 227–228.

[43] *Ac.*, II, 100.

[44] *M*, VII, 184.

Time is another factor affecting the question of the criterion. Occasionally circumstances do not allow more than a cursory survey of the facts. We may be forced to make a decision or to take action without delay. In these cases assent to a credible impression is legitimate without further effort to establish its truth. The conviction produced, though not always strong, provides a justifiable basis for belief and resultant action. For example, if a man, pursued by enemies, comes upon a ditch and senses that his enemies lie in ambush there, he quite properly assents to that impression, avoiding the ditch without taking time to investigate further. Yet on other occasions, time permitting, a more thorough inquiry may be necessary to warrant assent. A person who sees a coil of rope in an unlighted room jumps over it, immediately taking it to be a snake. Yet he is not justified in clinging to that belief, if circumstances permit a more careful examination of the facts. That is, noticing that the coil is motionless, he may suspect his initial impression, prod the object with a stick, and discover finally that it is no more than a rope.

Carneades' examples[45] make it clear that on his view there is no single authorization for our beliefs and assertions. Credible impressions are doubtless a necessary condition, but the circumstances surrounding these beliefs and statements will sometimes call for more elaborate support. He makes no attempt to spell out what constitutes adequate basis in all cases, but he does furnish some guidelines for sorting out the criteria appropriately used on different occasions.

CARNEADES' CRITERIA. The first and most general criterion, as already stated, is simply the credible impression ($\pi\iota\theta\alpha\nu\grave{\eta}$ $\phi\alpha\nu\tau\alpha\sigma\acute{\iota}\alpha$) with its intrinsic power to produce conviction. But Carneades goes on to say that experience does not consist of individual data, separate and dis-

---

[45] *Ibid.*, 186–189; *PH*, I, 227–228.

tinct; it is a complex of impressions that hang together "like the links of a chain." [46] If we look at a person, for example, we experience a variety of impressions in combination — impressions of personal qualities (size, shape, speech, color) and of external conditions (light, atmospheric conditions, nearby objects). This provides basis for Carneades' second criterion, the impression that is both credible and consistent (πιθανὴ καὶ ἀπερίσπαστος φαντασία). Impressions tend to reinforce one another, so that when each of the credible impressions in a complex fits with the rest, the experience as a whole is consistent. Thus we believe that this man is Socrates because of the worn cloak, conversation, size, shape, color, and the rest of the characteristically "Socratic" qualities. A concurrence of credible impressions constitutes a stronger sanction for an assertion than would be provided by a single impression considered in isolation. Just as a physician does not diagnose a disease on the basis of one symptom only but a concurrence of symptoms,

> . . . so too the Academic forms his judgment of truth by the concurrence of impressions, and when none of the impressions in the concurrence arouses in him a suspicion that it is false, he says that the experience is true.[47]

The quoted passage introduces a new factor affecting the application of criteria, namely, doubt. Should something in the complex of impressions cause us to question the experience, the criterion shifts appropriately, so that a more careful investigation is required to authorize a corresponding perceptual statement. It is important to note the emphasis put on having *reason* to doubt. If no relevant feature of experience arouses suspicion, the Academic "says that the experience is

---

[46] *M*, VII, 176–177.
[47] *Ibid.*, 179: οὕτω καὶ ὁ Ἀκαδημαϊκὸς τῇ συνδρομῇ τῶν φαντασιῶν ποιεῖται τὴν κρίσιν τῆς ἀληθείας, μηδεμιᾶς τε τῶν ἐν τῇ συνδρομῇ φαντασιῶν περισπώσης αὐτὸν ὡς ψευδοῦς λέγει ἀληθὲς εἶναι τὸ προσπῖπτον.

true." We must have specific reasons for doubting impressions that otherwise we are entitled to accept.

Suppose, however, that there is reason to question. An inconsistency is felt, a perceptual assertion challenged, or the experience important enough to merit fuller investigation. Carneades' third criterion is then relevant — the credible impression that is both consistent and tested (πιθανὴ καὶ ἀπερίσπαστος καὶ διεξωδευμένη φαντασία).[48] Besides consistency there are tests to determine the reliability of experience which pertain to circumstances of perception, that is, as relevant to percipient, object, and medium of perception. As many conditions as are necessary can be checked. For, as Sextus explains in his exposition,[49] just as is the practice in the assembly when we examine the qualifications of those aspiring to be magistrates or judges, so too in the case of perception we need to make sure, for example, that the percipient has good vision and that he is wide awake. We can also check to see that the atmosphere is clear, that the distance from which an object is viewed is not too great, that the object is not in motion or too small to be judged accurately. When the necessary circumstances have been tested, a perceptual assertion is justified. Tested experience is the most convincing and issues in the most final and authoritative judgments (τελειοτάτη κρίσις).

The criteria of truth can thus be ranked according to their capacity to produce conviction.[50] The suitability of the criterion employed depends on the circumstances of the perceptual utterance. As experience is subjected

[48] *Ibid.*, 182–184, 187–189.

[49] *Ibid.*, 182–183.

[50] The order of the last two criteria is reversed by Sextus at *PH*, I, 227–230. There the sequence is "credible," "tested," and "consistent." The latter sequence is perhaps not the most common one, but the order does not seem to be crucial. In the passage mentioned Sextus gives an example of an impression that is credible and tested but not consistent, viz., Admetus' impression of Alcestis after she is delivered by Heracles from Hades.

to more tests, our statements carry increasingly more weight; no limit is placed by Carneades on the amount of testing that may be necessary.[51]

An important consequence of this view, as noted earlier, is that any perceptual statement, regardless of its justification, may be false. Many assertions are justified, but none is immune from error, since no impression is cataleptic. Carneades was aware of this implication.[52] Since the criteria do not secure the conditions of truth, he held accordingly that nothing is "absolutely" a criterion of truth.[53] Acknowledging implicitly the gap between absolute certainty and justification, he drew a parallel distinction between absolute and qualified assent. Since there is no absolute criterion of truth, the Academic will not give unqualified assent to any perceptual statement, though he will give a qualified assent.[54] The stronger the support, the stronger his conviction. On the other hand, the mere possibility of error and the rare occasions on which mistakes do occur are not in themselves a sufficient reason to doubt impressions that as a general rule are reliable.

. . . for it happens as a fact that both our judgments and our actions are regulated by the standard of the general rule.[55]

---

[51] M, VII, 177, 181, 183, 188; PH, I, 227–228.

[52] πάντα εἶναι ἀκατάληπτα. PH, I, 226; Pr. Ev., XIV, 7, 736d. Cf. M, VII, 174–175.

[53] M, VII, 159: οὐδέν ἐστιν ἁπλῶς ἀληθείας κριτήριον, οὐ λόγος, οὐκ αἴσθησις, οὐ φαντασία, οὐκ ἄλλο τι τῶν ὄντων · πάντα γὰρ ταῦτα συλλήβδην διαψεύδεται ἡμᾶς. Bury's translation (Loeb Classical Library), "There is absolutely no criterion of truth," contradicts Carneades' entire doctrine.

[54] Ac., II, 59, 104; PH, I, 230; M, VII, 177–178. There was apparently some disagreement among Carneades' disciples as to the correct interpretation of his stand with respect to assent (Ac., II, 78). Arcesilaus had been less liberal on this point than Carneades and denied that assent was ever justified. (Ac., II, 59, 66–67; M, VII, 157; PH, I, 232; Pr. Ev., XIV, 4, 726d.)

[55] M, VII, 175: τῷ γὰρ ὡς ἐπὶ τὸ πολὺ τάς τε κρίσεις καὶ τὰς πράξεις κανονίζεσθαι συμβέβηκεν.

Commentary. The Academic doctrine is a remarkable effort to find a solution to the difficulties surrounding the criterion of truth. The problem to which Carneades addressed himself was implicit in the Stoic account of knowledge; and, it is important to note, his criteria provide a way out without disturbing the most fundamental presuppositions of the Stoic theory. The differences between Carneades and the Stoics are therefore relatively few, but they are of course crucial to Carneades' attempt to expose and avoid the weaknesses of the Stoic position. The most striking dissimilarities are brought into focus by Carneades' distinction between conditions and criteria of truth and by his emphasis, in locating the criteria, on the relations between impressions rather than on the character of any single impression.

A major deficiency of the Stoic criterion, as we have seen, was its failure to provide a reliable method of distinguishing between true and false impressions. The cataleptic impression functioned both as authorization for a knowledge claim and as guarantee of the truth of that claim. The point of the Stoic criterion seems to have been to draw attention to the sort of experience that is felt unquestionably to be true and, accordingly, to a corresponding class of perceptual statements for which no further justification is necessary. The character of the type of experience referred to is such that it cannot be doubted or questioned. This is in part to say that in such cases a person is entitled to base an assertion on his own immediate experience. That point was not disputed by the Academics. What Carneades did deny, however, was the additional claim that perceptual assertions accompanied by the sort of experience described *could not be false* and, further, that the authority of our perceptual assertions and our conviction of their truth rest solely on the character of a *single* impression.

Let us consider the first point of disagreement, namely, Carneades' insistence that though one's experience may be so compelling as to be impossible for *him* to question, the experience as such is not unquestionable. The reason for that contention, judging from his subsequent analysis of impressions, seems to have been the impossibility of making the comparison between impression and object necessary to establish the truth of the impression. Nevertheless, even apart from the absurdity of that task, there is no difficulty in thinking of cases in which it would be perfectly proper to doubt or question a first-hand report of experience, owing to its intrinsic implausibility or because of conflict with other reports of the same occurrence. Carneades' examples were designed to bring out that point. Suppose, then, that just those experiences that are intrinsically unquestionable on the Stoic account are in fact questioned. How can the Stoic convince an antagonist that his experience is more believable than that of the madman who thinks he is pursued by daemons? The Stoic theory provides no means of testing the truth of a perceptual statement, once it has been called into question. The only test is the quality of the experience itself, and that will be of no help in settling disagreements of fact.

This leads to Carneades' second point of difference, which is that the reliability of our perceptual experience cannot be determined solely by the quality of individual impressions. Since every case of perception, even the simplest, involves numerous impressions and we do not attend to each impression individually, the truth of the experience as a whole is determined not just by the force and clarity of impressions but also by the relations between them. This observation furnishes Carneades with a way of testing perceptual statements which is independent of the content of the experiences they describe. The tests of consistency and scrutiny of perceptual conditions provide a basis for deciding factual disputes. The Stoic attempt to redeem their own criterion along these lines, that is, by pointing to the conditions under which perceptual errors are made, ironically confirms the Academic doctrine instead of their own.

A question of interpretation arises when we consider Carneades' distinction between absolute and qualified assent, which is the outcome of his view that a perceptual statement may be justified yet false. Consider the following version of his meaning.

1. We can never *know* whether a perceptual statement is true.

2. We are justified in *believing* that some statements are true.

The translation brings out the traditional contrast between knowledge and belief. If it is a correct analogue of the distinction between the two sorts of assent, Carneades' theory entails that knowledge is impossible, whereas belief is warranted by the criteria of truth. But compare that interpretation of the distinction with an alternate pair of statements.

3. We can never *know for certain* whether a perceptual statement is true.

4. We can *know* that some statements are true by the criteria of truth.

The second version implies a distinction between knowledge and certainty, which might appear to reflect more accurately the distinction between conditions and criteria of truth. It is clear that of the four statements Carneades would endorse 2 and 3. The strongest claim is thus ruled out and the weakest accepted. But the most interesting question concerns 1 and 4. Since the criteria authorize a perceptual statement, we may ask whether being in the position to make a justifiable assertion counts as authorization for a knowledge claim. The criteria of truth may seem to point toward an acceptance of 4, but there is a stronger presumption in favor of 1. It is not likely that Carneades rejected the Stoic definition of knowledge, according to which 3 and 4 are incompatible. Absolute certainty (κατάληψις), according to the Stoics, is a necessary condition of knowledge, which they defined as firm assent to a cataleptic (καταληπτική) impression. The Academic criticism does not repudiate the Stoic definition of knowledge so much as it denies the existence of cataleptic impressions. The skepticism of Carneades is understandable only on the supposition that 4 is ruled out. And it is a reasonable conjecture that Carneades would not have accepted a definition of knowledge less rigorous than that of his predecessors. Such a departure from tradition would have been unprecedented. Nevertheless, a doctrine that detaches the criteria of truth from the ideal of certainty is surely pointing in that direction.

Since the degree of conviction and (by Carneades' criteria) the authority of perceptual statements are directly proportional to the extent to which these statements are able to pass certain specifiable tests, and since no test is constitutive of knowledge, it might be said that the criteria make up a doctrine of evidence. Carneades does not speak unambiguously of "evidence" for the truth of perceptual assertions, but there is reason to interpret him that way. He likens impressions by analogy to "witnesses" cross-examined in respect of their testimony, "symptoms" of a disease diagnosed by a physician, and "messengers" conveying a report.[56] Insofar as witnesses, symptoms, and messengers produce or constitute evidence of something's being the case, credible impressions by analogy are evidence for the truth of a perceptual assertion. These examples tend to support the interpretation that Carneades' criteria introduce the notion of evidence as reasonable ground for a perceptual assertion. That is, we are entitled to say a statement is true if, and only if, it is supported by credible experience of the sort specified by the crite-

---

[56] *Ibid.*, 163, 179, 184. The "symptom" analogy, however, may have been introduced by Sextus, who was a physician.

ria.[57] What it means for an assertion to be "supported by" experience is explained by the nature and degrees of credible experience, which is to say, it must appear true, be consistent, and in some cases also be tested. In short, the criteria authorize assertions by stipulating what counts as evidence for them.

A final question can be raised in connection with the Academic doctrine. A criterion must be accepted in order to function as such. What is there to recommend the criteria of truth proposed by Carneades? Having already noted some important respects in which Carneades' theory is superior to the Stoic view, we could perhaps venture an answer by reference to those features. Yet a different sort of response might be more appropriate. Criteria may be discerned rather than proposed, and there are indications that Carneades considered his criteria to be recommended by the virtue of actual use. In the first place, they are not technical but are intended to be employed in ordinary life.[58] The point of the criteria seems to be not to provide a systematic doctrine of truth but to sketch an informal method actually employed for deciding whether a given assertion or belief should be regarded as true (whether assent is justified) within the context of a whole network of beliefs already accepted as true. Carneades makes no attempt to give the criteria exact formulation or to furnish explicit rules for their application. He does not spell out the exact circumstances under which assent is warranted or specify degrees of "probability" to correspond with degrees of conviction. He merely outlines the kinds of circumstances that affect the proper

[57] Little is said about the conditions under which a statement may be said to be false. If the criteria of truth are not met, though not permissible to claim that a statement is true, it does not follow that it can justifiably be said to be false. Carneades' theory could be extended without difficulty to include the notion of "evidence against" a statement.

[58] ". . . criterion for the conduct of life and the attainment of happiness" (M, VII, 166).

application of criteria; the rest is left open. To be sure, the criterion must be appropriate to the circumstances, but if someone wants to know in advance what that means, that is, which criterion to employ on which occasion, the account is of little help. He is left to decide for himself. The suggestion seems to be that we all know when and how to employ the criteria of truth. Yet the factors affecting our decisions are as difficult to enumerate and classify as the circumstances encountered in life. If this interpretation is correct, then by discerning and advocating a criterion of truth that is already in use, Carneades, like the Pyrrhonists, is recommending adherence to the practices and conventions of ordinary life.

COMPARISON WITH EARLY PYRRHONISM

It is worth contrasting the Skepticism of the Academy with that of the early Pyrrhonists. They shared the conviction that sensory experience, though the source of our beliefs about the world, cannot insure the truth of these beliefs. Yet they saw different implications in that position. Pyrrhonists considered the insight to be sufficient reason for rejecting categorically all perceptual statements. No perceptual assertion (belief) is true or false. Their alternative seems to have been to recommend a different class of statements as acceptable. A simple translation from the form "It is . . ." into "It appears . . ." results in a class of sense statements descriptive of experience and no more. Since no perceptual statement is true or false, the Pyrrhonist suspends judgment about all alike.

There is no evidence, on the other hand, that Academic Skeptics advocated any linguistic reformulation of that sort. Their skeptical conclusions about the possibility of guaranteeing the truth of perceptual assertions did not tempt them to alter the form of those statements to solve the problem. Instead, they turned to the question of justifying claims whose certainty cannot be established. Many of our beliefs and utterances are justifiable, even though none is totally free from doubt. That is, according to Carneades, there are reasons for accepting (with qualification) some perceptual statements as true. Unlike the Pyrrhonists, Carneades granted the truth (and falsity) of perceptual statements and looked for criteria governing the application of these concepts. The object perceived is the external object (τὸ ἐκτὸς ὑποκείμενον), as contrasted with the Pyrrhonic phenomenon, and our impressions are representative of that object.[59]

One might be led to conclude otherwise from the testimony of Sextus Empiricus that Carneades' criterion is the "apparently true."[60] It would be mistaken to infer on those grounds, however, that Carneades held that sense statements are true, or even that such statements constitute evidence for perceptual statements. On the contrary, we have seen that Carneades' criteria are introduced as authority for claiming that perceptual statements are true. And evidence for a perceptual statement ("There is a snake in the cellar") is another perceptual statement ("I saw it when I opened the door") but not a sense statement ("There appears to me to be a snake in the cellar"). If the original claim is questioned, evidence is adduced. But the Carneadean evidence can also be questioned — in a way rather different from questioning a sense statement — for example, "What you saw was a coil of rope." In the event that the evidence is questioned, better reasons are required to justify the original assertion.

Carneades' criteria permit a qualified assent to the kind of statement that is wholly repudiated by the Pyrrhonists, the sort that refers beyond the data of sense to the *objects* of experience. Pyrrhonists advocate

---

[59] *Ibid.*, 160, 167, 170.

[60] *Ibid.*, 173: ἡ δὲ φαινομένη ἀληθὴς καὶ ἱκανῶς ἐμφαινομένη κριτήριόν ἐστι τῆς ἀληθείας κατὰ τοὺς περὶ τὸν Καρνεάδην. See also *Ibid.*, 408.

following existing conventions without assent, whereas
Academics abandon the requirement of absolute certainty as the sole warrant and justification of assent.[61]
That is, they are less rigorous in applying the Skeptic
principle of suspense of judgment.[62]

[61] *PH*, I, 226–227, 230, 233.

[62] This does not apply to Arcesilaus, however, who is said to
have been more "consistent" in withholding assent than Carneades (*Ac.*, II, 59; *PH*, I, 232; *M*, VII, 157).

4 * SKEPTICISM OF AENESIDEMUS

The critical philosophy of Aenesidemus goes back for its stimulus to the beginnings of the Skeptical inquiry articulated by Pyrrho and his immediate disciples. By continuing that trend begun by earliest Skeptics, Aenesidemus did much to establish Pyrrhonism as a genuine philosophic movement. The name of Aenesidemus is traditionally associated with "tropes" or "modes" (τρόποι), that is, critical arguments designed to bring about suspense of judgment (ἐποχή). These arguments, which form the basis of Pyrrhonic Skepticism, can be divided into two categories, each of which bears directly on our present epistemological inquiry. The Ten Tropes of ἐποχή make up an attack on traditional theories of knowledge; and the Eight Tropes of Cause, together with Aenesidemus' remarks about signs, amount to a repudiation of the causal explanations of his predecessors and contemporaries.

TEN TROPES OF ΕΠΟΧΗ

The Ten Tropes, attributed by authorities to Aenesidemus,[1] constitute a unique systematization of all skeptical arguments known to Greek philosophers. Accordingly, not all the arguments and examples are original. Many are present in the writings of Plato and Aristotle, and some were employed by earlier Skeptics. But the account given by Aenesidemus is the first attempt to bring together all philosophical considerations that seem to lead to skepticism with respect to our knowledge of the material world. The objective is to induce

[1] M, VII, 345; Vit., IX, 78–79, 87; Aristocles in Pr. Ev., XIV, 18, 760b. The latter speaks of only nine Tropes.

suspense of judgment by setting in opposition a multitude of conflicting beliefs and experiences. Aenesidemus consistently employs a single strategy to this end. After looking into the origin of these incompatible beliefs and experiences and uncovering the many perceptual conditions affecting them, he argues that there is no acceptable standard for deciding between them or determining their correctness. The skeptical conclusion follows: Though we can say how an object appears, we are not justified in making any claims about its real nature.

THE TROPES. Following is a brief summary of Aenesidemus' arguments in the order given by Sextus Empiricus.[2]

1. *Differences among animals.* The argument begins by asserting that animals, owing to observable differences among them, do not receive the same impressions[3] from the same objects. That is, it is reasonable to expect that diversities in manner of generation, growth, and bodily structure are accompanied by parallel differences in sense perception. To show the plausibility of this premise, Aenesidemus has at hand a sizable store of evidence.[4]

[2] *PH*, I, 36–164. A similar account, though much abridged and in a different order, is given by Diogenes Laertius (*Vit.*, IX, 78–89). The exposition that follows is necessarily selective and contains samples from the discussions of Sextus and Diogenes.

[3] The Stoic (and Academic) term "impression" (φαντασία) appears throughout the Tropes as expounded by Sextus and Diogenes. This need not be taken to imply that Aenesidemus endorsed the Stoic doctrine of impressions as such. The term does not occur with the same frequency in Photius' summary of Aenesidemus' philosophy (*Bibliotheca*, Cod. 212, 169–170). Nevertheless, there is little doubt that Aenesidemus drew a similar distinction between experience and object, because the force of the Tropes, regardless of the language in which they are stated, rests on such a contrast. A distinction closely parallel to the Stoic "impression-object" is accordingly presupposed by the discussion in the present section.

[4] It would be unnecessarily tedious to try to include all the examples (many of which are factually wrong) presented by Sextus

The eyes of animals vary noticeably in size, shape, and color. Some are small, others large; some are dark, others luminous enabling the animal to see in the dark. Cats and certain other creatures have elongated pupils, as contrasted with those animals whose pupils are round. Some eyes are convex, protruding beyond the face; others appear flat and still others concave. If we recall the effects produced by convex and concave mirrors, we may expect that the visual experiences of these animals vary similarly. Therefore it is reasonable to suppose that,

> . . . dogs, fishes, lions, men, and locusts do not see the same objects either as the same size or as of similar shape, but that the visual organ receiving the phenomenon affects the nature of the imprint formed of each thing.[5]

Much the same can be said of the other sense organs. It is unlikely that creatures covered variously with scales, shells, feathers, and flesh all have the same tactile experiences. So too with the senses of hearing, taste, and smell. Auditory organs, for example, are observed to differ among animals. Just as the sound of a flute can be made to vary in accordance with the length and shape of the passage through which the breath flows, it is probable that the auditory sensations of creatures are determined by the different structures of their corresponding organs. The same conclusion seems to follow from noticing the preferences and aversions of animals. Pleasure and pain are derived from sense impressions, and it is generally agreed that what brings pleasure to one animal may cause pain to another. In the light of these diversities it is safe to infer that the same objects do not produce the same impressions in animals differing markedly in bodily structure.

Having established that point, Aenesidemus goes on

---

and Diogenes. Nevertheless, all those that do appear in the present account of the Tropes are taken from the texts.

[5] *PH*, I, 49.

to say that we have no good reason to regard the sense impressions of the human animal, in preference to those of other creatures, as disclosing the real nature of an object. To do so would be arbitrary. The senses of human beings are not always the most acute. Hawks have sharper vision than men, and dogs a keener sense of smell. We have no objective standard to allow us to say that a certain set of sense impressions, as opposed to some other, reveals the actual constitution of the world. It follows that we may say how an object appears, but not what its real nature is. In regard to that we can only suspend judgment.

2. *Differences among human beings.* The second Trope argues along similar lines, except that the stress is on physical and psychic differences among human beings. Even if it be granted that experiences and beliefs of men are more trustworthy than those of other animals, we are still at a loss to decide which man's impressions are more believable than the next. It is likely that the way human beings experience the world is a function of their constitutional differences, which in turn are determined by the prevailing "humors" of the body. And these physical and psychic differences are reflected in the diverse preferences and aversions characteristic of different persons.

> Since, therefore, choice and avoidance are dependent on pleasure and displeasure, and pleasure and displeasure on sensation, that is, sense impression, whenever some men choose the same things that are avoided by others, as a consequence we conclude that they are not similarly affected by the same things, since otherwise they would have chosen and avoided the same things.[6]

Again, because there is nothing to choose between different impressions of the same thing, we are able to say how an object appears to us in relation to these con-

[6] *Ibid.,* I, 87.

stitutional differences, but not what it really is in its own nature.

3. *Different constitution of sense organs.* Disparate impressions of the same object are received via the several senses, owing to their differing constitutions. Sometimes these impressions are wholly incommensurate, as when taste reports that an object is sweet; sight that it is neither sweet nor sour but, say, red; and touch, none of the foregoing, but perhaps rough or smooth. On occasion the data of different senses are even incompatible, as when a painting appears to the eye to have recesses and projections, but not to touch. Moreover, some things appear pleasant to one sense, but unpleasant to another. Perfume, for example, though pleasing to smell, has a disagreeable taste.

As a result of these disparities we think of objects as complexes or aggregates of qualities. The apple appears smooth, fragrant, sweet, and yellow. But we have no way of knowing whether it has just those qualities, or perhaps more or less. It may in reality have only one quality but appear variously because of the different structures of the five sense organs. Or perhaps the reverse. It may have more qualities than appear to us. Our knowledge is limited by sense, just as the knowledge of a man born deaf and blind is limited to a fraction of reality. The apple may possess qualities other than those known to us — qualities that could be perceived with the aid of an appropriate sense organ. We are thus forced to suspend judgment as to the real nature of an object whose apparent nature only is manifest to sense.

4. *Conditions affecting subject.* This argument enumerates a list of subjective conditions that play a part in determining the character of perceptual experience. For instance, men who are mad or inspired are known to have experiences unlike the normal. Wholesome food often tastes bitter to the sick, and lukewarm water seems hot when poured on an inflamed area of the skin. These abnormal experiences can doubtless be explained

by certain combinations of bodily "humors," but the same can be said of normal experience. It is also a product of a particular mixture of these fluids. Age too is a factor altering the character of experience; a breeze that seems mild to a youth may feel cold to an older person. Moreover, our impressions are affected by local motion and rest. Objects that appear at rest when we are standing still seem to be in motion when we move past them. Other conditions, such as hunger and drunkenness, are known to affect perceptual experience, and strong emotions bring about similar changes. Love and hatred, grief and joy, fear and confidence cause us to experience the world variously at different times, for we seldom sustain a single emotion for a long period without feeling conflicting ones. In light of these considerations, which experiences are to count as revealing the true character of the world? No matter what impressions are accepted as accurate, all are conditioned by some state, whether it be health, illness, drunkenness, sobriety, or something else. Most frequently persuaded by present experience, we are in no position to make an accurate judgment. A man who has drunk too much wine is convinced that he possesses a superior awareness, but when sober he dismisses his previous "insights" as unsound. The most compelling dream is discounted on awaking as fictitious and illusory. Since there is no objective standard enabling us to measure the accuracy of impressions independently of these states, we must suspend judgment as to the real constitution of things, being content to affirm experienced phenomena.

5. *Position, distance, location of object.* The content of experience is influenced by circumstances surrounding the object. The same porch appears to have different shapes according to the position from which it is viewed. A pigeon's neck varies in color depending on the degree to which it is inclined toward or away from the observer. The same ship seen from a distance appears small and motionless, but large and in motion

from up close. Sound produced in a pipe is unlike the sound proceeding from a flute, and an oar presents different appearances in and out of the water. There is no justification for preferring one set of impressions over another as revealing the character of the object.

> Since, therefore, all phenomena are perceived in something and from a certain distance or in a certain position, and each of these circumstances causes a great variation in the impressions, as we have observed, we shall be forced through this Trope, too, to end by suspending judgment.[7]

6. *Admixtures intrinsic to perception.* Objects do not affect the senses by themselves alone but always in conjunction with something else. The experienced object is thus a resultant mixture not identical with the object in its pure state. The color of a man's complexion, for example, varies with temperature. It appears one color in warm air and another in cold. Since it is always perceived at some temperature, however, what is actually seen is the man's complexion, not in itself, but only as it is affected by varying temperatures. Similarly, sounds and odors are always experienced in conjunction with a rare or dense atmosphere, so that in these cases too it is the complex phenomenon that is actually perceived. Other perceptual admixtures are internal. The eye contains membranes and fluids in conjunction with which visual sensations occur. Saliva is a fluid always present to taste, and other substances are intrinsic to the remaining sense organs. For these reasons we are able to describe the ultimate product of all these admixtures, whereas we can say nothing of the object in itself.

7. *Quantity and composition of object.* The quantity and composition of things also affect the character of experience. Silver filings appear black when viewed separately, but white when united in a mass. A chip of marble looks white by itself but yellow as part of a large block. Scattered pebbles present a coarse or jagged

---

[7] *Ibid.,* I, 121.

appearance to the eye, whereas a large heap of the same stones looks soft. We can describe the appearances of silver (black or white), marble (white or yellow), and pebbles (rough or soft), but we cannot say what their real nature is because of the variations in our sense impressions. Food and wine, moreover, have markedly different effects when taken in large or small quantities. In general, wholesome things become harmful when used immoderately, as is the case with medicine and drugs. These facts also add to the difficulties surrounding the real nature of the object, with respect to which the Skeptic therefore suspends judgment.

8. *Relations.* Since all objects of perception are affected by their relations to a percipient and to accompanying circumstances, it is impossible, apart from these relations, to grasp the character of the object itself. Sextus in his exposition singles out the eighth Trope as the most important. Arguments based on the existence of relations comprise a class including all the rest of the Tropes as members. That is, the force of all the arguments rests on the epistemological relation between subject and object. Each Trope details specific conditions that affect this relation and hence our perceptual experience. Certain Tropes emphasize conditions affecting subject; others, those affecting object. But in each case the important relation between knower and object known is central to the argument. The Skeptic concludes that we can say nothing of the nature of the object as it exists independently of these relations.

9. *Effects of frequent and rare occurrences.*[8] Familiarity and abundance have a significant effect on our judgments about things. The sun, for example, which is seen every day, causes no amazement in anyone, but a comet, a rare occurrence, occasions so much wonder

[8] Tropes 9 and 10 look into the multitude of factors that generate and shape values. The assumption is that judgments of value, like ordinary perceptual statements, make claims about the real properties of things. Hence, they both invite the same sort of criticism.

as even to be considered a divine portent. Other natural phenomena, such as earthquakes and the sea, cause less excitement in those accustomed to them than in those who experience them for the first time. In the same way we come to regard rare objects as precious and common things as worthless. If gold were scattered in great abundance over the earth, it is safe to say that no one would consider it worth hoarding. Again it follows that we are able to say how an object appears to us in virtue of its frequent or rare occurrence, but we can make no statement about its true nature.

10. *Effects of laws, habits, customs.* Standards of taste and morality are largely determined by law, custom, and tradition, which are generally acknowledged to vary among different peoples.[9] What is considered unseemly, immoral, or irreligious by one group is accepted as fitting and right by another. Judgments of value therefore cannot be counted as descriptive of the real nature of things, since they are a product of habitation, training, and education.

Commentary. The foregoing Tropes set forth an impressive array of circumstances affecting perceptual experience. Each argument claims to show that the manifold conditions involved in perception make it impossible to grasp the real character of the world. The strategy is roughly the same throughout.[10] Our impressions of an object are first observed to vary according to different perceptual conditions, each Trope stressing the effect of a particular set of conditions on perceptual experience. Because of this variation, it is argued, we can say how an object appears to us but not what it is in its real nature. To determine the force of the Tropes

---

[9] There follows a long list of diverse practices and customs, which would be tiresome to repeat. See *PH*, I, 145–164.

[10] In the preceding exposition I have set forth what I take to be the most important argument in each Trope. The central argument, however, is frequently accompanied by other less interesting ones that I have not included, both for the sake of clarity and to keep the discussion within manageable limits.

it is necessary to look more closely at the structure of the arguments and examine some of the key terms that recur. The following schema (A) represents one pattern of reasoning that occurs repeatedly in Sextus' exposition.

1. The same objects appear different (different impressions are produced by the same objects) owing to differences in perceptual conditions.

[2. The real nature of an object is independent of perceptual conditions.]

3. We have no criterion to determine the accuracy of one perceptual experience (set of impressions) over another.

4. We can say how an object appears to us (describe our impressions), but not what it is in its real nature, i.e., we do not know the real nature of the object.

(A1) — By far the greatest attention of the Tropes is devoted to establishing the first premise of the argument. An exhaustive list of examples is cited to show that perceptual experiences can be made to vary as the relevant conditions under which perception takes place are altered. The premise is intended to state a fact of experience, and it is supported by actual cases of sensory variation. That is, a person upon leaving the bath reports that the air that seems mild to others feels chilly to him. The object that looked small from a distance looks larger when it is approached. And similarly with the rest of the examples. They are intended (with obvious exceptions, such as the analogies in the first Trope) to record observable differences that can be confirmed (or falsified) by our own experiences and by the reports of other persons. So much, then, is the substance of (A1). But Sextus' exposition introduces other considerations, which, though apparently secondary and not essential to the argument as a whole, deserve mention.

The first concerns the existence of incompatible beliefs about the same object. The Tropes stress, in varying degrees, the existence of conflicting opinions and beliefs. The emphasis placed on this kind of disagreement is both instructive and misleading—instructive because it points to an assumption that pervades the Tropes, and misleading because it suggests that the existence of such conflict of opinion is essential to the main argument. The last two Tropes in particular, since they are concerned with judgments of the value or worth of objects, institutions, and practices, make much of these conflicts of belief. Tropes 9 and 10 quite naturally begin by noting the wide divergencies in belief with regard to aesthetic, ethical, religious, and other social matters, rather than by pointing to differences in perceptual experience as is the practice in the other Tropes. But the argument then proceeds along familiar lines by denying any basis for preferring one set of beliefs over another. The two-fold assumption underlying the argument of the last Tropes is as follows: First, different impressions (of worth, value) are produced by the same objects (practices, institutions) owing to relevant differences of circumstance (frequency of occurrence, abundance, habit, education, and the like); and, second, these different impressions generate different (and incompatible) beliefs about the same things, not all of which can be true. It is important to note that both parts of the assumption pervade all the Tropes, which treat judgments of value much on a par with ordinary perceptual statements. To say, for example, that an object is beautiful is, in an important sense, like saying that it is rough or smooth. In each case a statement is made about the real nature of the object, and in neither case is it justified. Conflicting value judgments, like conflicting perceptual statements, indicate that we are affected differently by things in the world, and this diversity in sense impressions gives rise to incompatible beliefs.[11] The structure of the argument in the last two Tropes, contrary to its surface appearance, does not differ from the rest, in which differences of opinion are not stressed.

[11] *PH*, I, 85–89, 96, 106, 141–164.

The original disparity in all the Tropes is with sense impressions, divergencies in belief being indicative of such differences in sensory experience. This explains the formulation of the first premise as in (A1), rather than in terms of conflicting beliefs, which are derivative in the sense mentioned and hence not necessary to a statement of the argument's structure. On the other hand, it is clear that the Skeptic argument would be weakened to the extent that it is made dependent on the assumption that different perceptual experiences invariably generate incompatible beliefs. For though there may be a perceptual belief (statement) corresponding to every perceptual experience, it is false that we always hold beliefs exactly corresponding to our sense impressions. The oar may look bent when immersed in water, but few would believe on that basis that it really is bent. To suppose that our beliefs are exact replicas of sensory experience is naïve; but the main argument of the Tropes, as stated in Sextus' exposition, is independent of such a supposition and requires as the initial premise no more than a statement, as in (A1), recording diversities in sense impressions, which in point of fact may or may not generate conflicting beliefs.

Another factor that tends to obscure rather than clarify the issue in the Tropes is the unnecessary reliance sometimes placed on the existence of different preferences and aversions as a means of establishing premise (A1). Thus Sextus in his exposition urges the fact that some persons (animals) choose just those things that are avoided by others as evidence that they are affected differently by the same things, that is, they have different impressions of the same objects. It is not surprising to find these considerations introduced in the first Trope where the subject discussed is differences among animals. But it is misleading to introduce the same reasoning into the Tropes that deal primarily with the different perceptual experiences of persons.[12] For

[12] For example, at *PH*, I, 80, 87, 106, 108. The last two Tropes

there is no need to rely on, as a basis for inference, different preferences and aversions, which in any event could not establish (A1), when the firsthand reports of percipients are available. The fact of different preferences and aversions, therefore, can be bypassed in setting forth the main argument of the Tropes, since (A1) can be established merely by the reports of percipients whose perceptual experiences differ.

(A2) — The second premise is not explicitly stated in the Tropes but is assumed throughout. The character of the object itself is independent of the perceptual conditions that account for differences in our impressions of it. The implication here is that not all impressions of an object can be veridical. It would be contradictory to assert that the stick really is both straight and bent, though it may appear to have incompatible properties, depending on the circumstances in which it is viewed.[18] If some of the properties that appear to characterize an object do not actually belong to it, then some impressions do not represent the object accurately.

(A3) — The third statement raises the question of deciding which impressions, if any, are accurate representations of the object. Since experience is conditioned by the physical structure of the percipient, his mental state, his training, physical circumstances of the object, and since these conditions are not uniform, persons often have diverse impressions and beliefs about the world. At this point Aenesidemus maintains that there is no objective or impartial (εἰλικρινής) standard to decide between conflicting impressions and rival accounts of the same thing. For we have no justification for selecting one set of impressions over another as disclosing the nature of the object. We cannot make an impartial de-

---

frequently mention different preferences and aversions, but there the subject is conflicting value judgments. As stated above, these are not clearly distinguished from ordinary perceptual statements.

[18] See, for example, *PH*, I, 88, where it is said that we cannot accept everyone's impressions, for that would involve accepting contradictory beliefs or assertions (τὰ ἀντικείμενα).

cision, since whatever experience is singled out is a product of the very factors over which, by its means, we would then presume to stand as judge.[14] The claim that there is no justifiable basis for deciding between impressions quite obviously intends to rule out the possibility of a purely rational solution to the problem. That is, reason cannot make such a decision, because it has no direct access to the truth independent of sensory experience.[15] Since the materials of thought are ultimately the data of sense, all decisions of reason are infected with the same blindness or bias that characterizes experience.

It is clear that on this account experience is a simple sequential occurrence of sense impressions, and all impressions are intrinsically of equal authority. It will therefore not do to argue that although experience is contingent on the existence of sense organs, physical and mental dispositions, and the like, some conditions are accepted as standard or normal; and that, given this fact, we never have any trouble distinguishing between veridical and illusory experience in spite of the Skeptic claim. Such an objection does not meet Aenesidemus' argument. The question at issue is not whether we do in fact accept certain perceptual conditions as standard, but whether perception under these conditions discloses the character of the external object. If all experience is affected by the many conditions enumerated in the Tropes, what justification is there for accepting certain conditions as standard or normal? Any criterion selected from experience begs the very question at issue.

> . . . just as healthy persons are in a state that is natural for the healthy but unnatural for the sick, so too those who are sick are in a state that is unnatural for the healthy but natural for the sick.[16]

[14] *PH*, I, 112–113, 121, 140.
[15] *PH*, I, 128: "But neither does the mind [apprehend the real object] especially since its guides, which are the senses, go wrong." See also *Ibid.*, 99.
[16] *Ibid.*, 103.

(A4) — The conclusion of the Tropes is that we have no criterion of veridical experience, and hence we do not know the real nature of the object. Any experience proposed is rejected as arbitrary, since there is no reason to believe that one set of impressions is more accurate than another. If experience is to count as veridical, it must reveal the object rather than its appearances. In short, the phenomenon perceived must be identical with the object. Since we have no way of determining whether or not this is the case, we must suspend judgment regarding the real nature of the object, making no claims that go beyond a description of impressions.

What, then, is the force of the contention that we can say how an object appears, but not what its real nature is? We can come up with no answer to this question without first looking carefully at the meanings of several terms that recur in the argument. Perhaps the most important of these is "real (external) object."[17]

The pattern of reasoning represented in schema (A) indicates that the real object is identical with some (unspecified) set of perceptible qualities, that is, some set of appearances (phenomena) or possible appearances. Alternately, to use the language of impressions, the real object consists of just those properties matched by some (correct) set of impressions. This interpretation is suggested by numerous passages in Sextus' text, where the "same object," as expressed in (A1), seems to be assimilated to the common objects of perceptual experience. Thus it is said (at 101) that the same water appears both lukewarm and very hot when in contact

---

[17] The following terms that occur in the text (*PH*, I, 40–164) I have, up to this point, translated more or less interchangeably (depending on the context) by "object," "real object," "real properties," "real nature," and "external object:" τὸ ὑποκείμενον (46, 47, 58, 59, 78, 87, 102, 106, 112, 124, 163), τὸ ἐκτος (ὑποκείμενον) (48, 61, 80, 99, 113, 117, 124, 128, 134, 144, 163), τὸ πρᾶγμα (59, 101, 107, 118, 140, 144), ἡ φύσις (59, 78, 87, 93, 117, 128, 132, 134, 135, 140, 163). These terms are usually contrasted with τὸ φαινόμενον and ἡ φαντασία.

with an inflamed area of the skin. The same honey (101) tastes sweet to the healthy and bitter to the sick. The same ship (118) appears small and stationary from a distance and large and in motion from up close. The same marble (130) appears yellow in a block but white when chipped off. The objects in these examples are the familiar items denoted by the terms "water," "honey," "ship," and "marble." Our impressions of these objects vary depending on the conditions under which they are perceived. Nevertheless (premise (A2)), the object itself (its real character) does not vary in a similar fashion, but remains what it is regardless of the circumstances that affect our impressions of it. It follows, therefore, that not all impressions can represent the object accurately (not all phenomena can be identical with the object). The problem posed by (A3) is one of determining which of the qualities perceived are the real ones. Thus we find it articulated in the Tropes as one of choosing between impressions or giving the preference ($\pi\rho o\kappa\rho i\nu\epsilon\iota\nu$) to one set of impressions over another.[18] If the difficulty is that of choosing between impressions (deciding between phenomena), this suggests that some choice would be the correct one. That is, some set of impressions reveals the nature of the object (some set of appearances is identical with the object). The real properties of the object, therefore, are those perceived under certain preferred conditions, but not necessarily those characteristically involved in perception by human beings. The preferred conditions will of course be those that render impressions exact replicas of the object (those that result in phenomena identical with the object). Since the difficulty stated in (A3) involves a criterion of veridical experience, we can ask what would count as a justifiable basis for deciding between impressions. And the Tropes contain an unambiguous answer to this question.[19] The disparity between

---

[18] See, for example, *PH*, I, 61, 78, 90, 114, 122.
[19] See especially Tropes 4 and 8 (*PH*, I, 112–114, 135–136).

impressions admits of no settlement, for no one is in a position to be an impartial judge of his sense impressions. All experience is necessarily conditioned by some state belonging to the specific constitution of the percipient. Thus whether we are in good or ill health, awake or asleep, old or young, mad or sane, our impressions of the object are modified by these conditions and confused by them. It follows that we can never make an impartial decision with respect to the accuracy of impressions, since we are never in a position to compare impressions with the objects so as to discover the degree of resemblance between them. To be able to make such a comparison entails being untouched by the very conditions that define perception itself. It is, therefore, impossible in principle to justify the preference of one criterion of veridical experience over any other, for any criterion selected begs the question of real existence. To know the real nature of an object it is necessary to "verify" our impressions by comparing them with the object itself, and that of course is impossible. Given the nature of the problem, then, as embodied in (A3), it is clear that the sense of "real object" in the argument has undergone a subtle change. The real object of the conclusion (A4) — that is, the object that cannot be known — is not merely some unspecified set of appearances but some *unspecifiable* set of appearances, the unspecifiability here being a matter of theoretical impossibility.

There is also, however, a second sense of "real object" that can be detected in the Tropes. It is most evident in the sixth (admixtures) but also is relevant to Tropes 3 (constitution of sense organs) and 8 (relations). The sixth Trope argues that the external object affects the organs of sense always in conjunction with something else, for example, atmospheric conditions and "membranes and fluids" of the sense organs, with the result that the object assumes a different appearance because of these accompanying media. The consequence is that the nature of what is perceived (phenomenon) is determined not just by the external object but also by the media in which perception takes place,

> . . . so that because of these admixtures, the senses do not apprehend in all accuracy the character of the external object.[20]

Trope 3 contains the similar suggestion that the senses actually prevent apprehension of the real nature of the object.[21] The implication here seems to be that the real object is not (cannot be) identical with *any* set of appearances, or alternately that *no* set of impressions can match the object. That is to say, it is something that exists independently of all perceptual conditions; but any set of perceptual conditions alters its character, so that the object as perceived is necessarily different from the object in its real nature. The very relation to a percipient or knowing subject distorts it.[22] "Real object," therefore, according to this interpretation and as it appears in the conclusion of certain Tropes, designates an entity that exists independently of all perceptual (and cognitive) conditions. It is clearly impossible to know the character of such an object because of the very conditions that define the knowing relation. Corresponding to this second sense of "real object" in the Tropes is the following modification (B) of the pattern of reasoning represented in schema (A):

> 1. The same objects appear different owing to differences in perceptual conditions (appearances of an object are a function of perceptual conditions).
> [2. The real nature of an object is independent of perceptual conditions.]

---

[20] *PH*, I, 127.

[21] *PH*, I, 95: "for it is possible also that the apple is of a single character (μονοειδές) but merely appears differentiated owing to differences in the sense organs in which perception takes place." See also the objection to "Nature made the senses commensurate with the objects of sense" at 98.

[22] In the fourth Trope (103) it is suggested that the prevailing "humors" of the body have a μεταβλητικὴ δύναμις.

3. We are acquainted in experience only with appearances of objects.

4. We can say how an object appears to us, but not what it is in its real nature, i.e., we do not know the real nature of the object.

(B1) — The first premise of the Skeptic argument as stated in schema (B) is like its counterpart in (A), except that it must be interpreted to mean not only that experience of an object is affected by diverse perceptual conditions, but further that the perceptual object itself is in some measure defined or constituted by these conditions. That is, the conditions under which perception takes place play a part in bringing into existence and shaping the character of the perceptual object. This shift in meaning makes (B1) look much less like an empirical claim than (A1). Though (A1) is supported by unlike reports of percipients, (B1) insofar as it makes the stronger claim cannot be confirmed or (falsified) by descriptions of phenomena. Nevertheless, the facts of experience are not irrelevant to (B1). Changes in the "membranes and fluids" of the sense organs along with variations in external media of perception, such as atmospheric conditions, could perhaps be observed to bring about corresponding changes in the quality of sensory experience. Yet no empirical test can be devised to measure the effects of the sorts of perceptual conditions mentioned (internal and external media) on the quality of sensory experience *as such*. Indeed, it hardly makes sense to speak of "testing" the effects of the very conditions that make perception possible. Nevertheless, the stronger claim that perceptual conditions play a part in bringing the perceptual object into existence is very likely intended to be an inference based on the weaker (empirical) statement that certain variations in the media of perception are accompanied by noticeable changes in our experience.

(B2) — The ground is now prepared for the second (suppressed) premise of the argument, which states that

the real character of the object is independent of perceptual conditions. That is, "real nature" defines the
object as it exists apart from the countless relations involved in its being perceived. The force of (B2), when
it is taken in conjunction with (B1), is to disallow that
the real nature of an object can ever be identical with
its phenomenal or perceived character, regardless of
what conditions obtain in the perceptual situation.

(B3) — The implication of (B1) and (B2) is that we
are never acquainted in experience with the real object
but only with its appearances. Since the character of
experience is affected by changes in perceptual circumstances, whereas the real nature of the object is not so
influenced and, indeed, is necessarily different from
phenomena, it follows that the object of our experience
is never the real object but only phenomena (its appearances). The very conditions that make perception
possible make veridical perception impossible. Our impressions can never be exact likenesses of the object, for
impressions owe their existence to a perceptual situation that is necessarily excluded by the concept of "real
object."

(B4) — The Skeptic therefore concludes that we can
say how an object appears, but we can say nothing of
its real nature. To know the real character of the object
is theoretically impossible, just as it was shown to be
in Schema (A), but in the present case the problem is
not one of comparing impressions and object for purposes of judging accuracy, but instead, of apprehending
the object independently of the conditions that define
the perceptual (and cognitive) relation.

Here again the conclusion rests on the supposition
that reason has no privileged access to the truth. That
is, in our rational deliberations and judgments we deal
exclusively with data of sense, so that mind is subject
to the same distortion that intrinsically mars sense perception.[23] The next step toward determining the effec-

[23] Cf. n. 15.

tiveness of the Tropes is to take a closer look at this assumption.

The view that reason cannot grasp realities inaccessible to sense seems to derive from what we have already referred to as an "empiricist axiom" endorsed by Skeptics, namely, that knowledge has its origin in sensory experience. As noted previously, Aenesidemus implies in the Tropes that reason has not the capacity to apprehend external realities by itself alone but is limited to dealing in various ways with the data or information made available to it through the sensory apparatus. If we are to come to know the nature of an object, sense experience will be a necessary condition (causally) of this knowledge. It also seems correct to interpret the Skeptic as saying, moreover, that sense experience (someone's having impressions of an object) is a (logically) necessary condition of establishing the truth of any statement about that existing thing. Now if sense experience both is, in the above ways, a necessary condition of knowledge and is, at the same time, as shown by the reasoning in (A) and (B), the very factor that makes knowledge of an object impossible, it is easy to see that there is no way out of the Skeptic predicament, unless reason can be called in to solve the difficulty. It is therefore relevant to ask whether reason, granted that it has no independent access to the real world, cannot purify the reports of sense in some other manner. That is, is it not possible to make allowances for the distortions of sense by controlled observations, measurements of perceptual variation, and theories designed to eliminate factors responsible for perceptual error? There is no doubt that the Skeptic conclusion as stated in (A4) and (B4) dictates a negative response to this question. Judgments of reason are necessarily contaminated by the same errors and confusions found in sense perception. To correct the errors of sense, reason would have to be, in the one case (A), in a position to compare impressions with their objects and, in the other (B), able to apprehend an object unconditioned by any perceptual or cognitive relations. The Skeptic conclusion in both (A) and (B) rests on the theoretical impossibility of apprehending the external object—an impossibility generated by the very conditions that define the knowing relation.

We are now in a better position to evaluate the Skeptic claim that we can say (know) nothing of the real nature of an object. In view of the innumerable examples of diverse perceptual experiences cited in the Tropes in support of that assertion, it is likely that it is intended to be an established factual claim. The first premise of the argument in both (A) and (B) states that the same objects appear different owing to differences in perceptual conditions. This is intended to be, and is, with the exceptions and reservations already mentioned in connection with (A1) and (B1) respectively, a statement about observable differences in the character of the experiences reported by percipients in varying circumstances (the same breeze feels cold to one, mild to another). We may inquire, however, to what extent the Skeptic conclusion is actually supported by the examples put forth. It is fairly clear that on either interpretation (A) or (B), no case taken from experience can count as knowing the real properties of the object. No set of conditions can be devised so as to result in knowledge of the real instead of mere acquaintance with the apparent. For the conditions necessary to knowing are the same that make knowledge impossible. The impossibility in schema (A) was that of comparing impressions (or appearances) with objects and in schema (B) our inability to apprehend the object independently of the media of impressions (independently of appearances). But if no actual or possible (given the conditions that limit the knowing relation) experience counts as a case of knowing the object, then the claim that we can say nothing of the real properties of objects cannot be falsified by any empirical means. Yet if that is the case, neither can it be confirmed by reference to actual cases from experience. The implication for the Tropes therefore is apparent. None of the factual examples of diverse impressions of the same object cited in the Tropes, summarized in (A1) and (B1), actually supports the conclusion that we do not know the real nature of the object. The reason for this oddity is that, whereas all the examples of objects appearing different under different conditions in (A1) and (B1) are taken from experience (that is, the objects themselves are *identifiable* parts of our experience), the two meanings of "(real) object" that have already been elicited from the Tropes and that appear respectively in conclusions (A4) and (B4) are such that *nothing* in experience can count as a (real) object. This is obvious in (B4), but it is also true in (A4) where, though the (real) object is identical with some set of appearances (phenomena), it cannot be recognized, pointed out, or otherwise identified as any particular set of appearances. Consequently, the objects that *appear different* are not (B), or cannot be said to be (A), identical with the *unknowable* entities referred to in the conclusion, for the latter are not (or cannot be said to be) designated by the terms customarily used to refer to the objects of experience. Corresponding to the one set of entities, which are said to appear different under different circumstances, are object words with the conventional meanings of ordinary discourse, and to the other, terms with the two philosophical senses we have elicited. It is clear that statements about the familiar items of ordinary experience cannot support or establish the truth of statements about external (real) objects.[24]

[24] It is equally important to notice that the identifiable object that "appears different" in the premise of the argument cannot be assimilated to the Skeptic phenomenon either. The identity of the former is logically independent of how it appears (its appearances), while the identity of a phenomenal object is not. The phenomenon is an appearance; as such it cannot appear different, nor can there be different appearances of it. Not surprisingly, the effectiveness of the argument of the Tropes depends in large measure on the ambiguity that results from blurring all these distinctions. A few passages in Sextus' account use the sub-

An interesting consequence follows from the above analysis. The conclusion of Aenesidemus' Tropes is that we can say how an object appears but not what it really is. It is not unreasonable to suppose that this statement contains an implicit recommendation. That is, we ought not to make assertions of the form, "X (really) is Y," but instead limit ourselves to the form, "X appears Y," because we cannot know (say) the real nature of an object. Consider the following three statements.

1. We do not know (cannot say) that any object (X) (really) is of a certain character (Y).
2. Dion knows (can say) that the honey (really) is sweet.
3. Theon does not know (cannot say) that the honey (really) is sweet.

What is the relation between 2 and 3, which are ordinary assertions about Dion, Theon, and honey, and 1, which is the philosophical conclusion of the Tropes? It looks as if 1 is contradicted by 2 and supported by 3, but in fact this is not the case. Statements 2 and 3 concern an identifiable object (the honey), whereas 1 is about external objects and says nothing whatever about the object of statements 2 and 3. Consequently, if the Skeptic conclusion is an implicit recommendation, it is not applicable to statements about the familiar items of ordinary experience. Its truth is not contingent on matters of fact but is a necessary consequence of the meanings of the terms as they are employed. It says, in effect, that we cannot know the character of an object

---

stantive φαινόμενον to refer to the identifiable object of experience, e.g., 49, 90, and especially 94–95 and 121. But most passages have (apparently interchangeably) (ἐκτὸς) ὑποκείμενον or πρᾶγμα for both what I have distinguished as the identifiable object (in the premise of the argument) and the real but unknowable object (in the conclusion). Cf., e.g., 48, 58, 59, 61, 78, 99, 101, 107, 113, 118, 124, 140, 144. A typical locution which veils and hence preserves the ambiguity necessary to the argument, is (78): ὁποῖον μὲν ἕκαστον τῶν ὑποκειμένων ἐμοὶ φαίνεται δυνήσομαι λέγειν, ὁποῖον δὲ ἔστι τῇ φύσει διὰ τὰ προειρημένα ἐπέχειν ἀναγκασθήσομαι.

independently of the conditions that make it (for us) knowable.

The Skeptic conclusion, therefore, is misleading to the extent that it appears to conflict with ordinary perceptual assertions about the properties of objects. Still, it is not for this reason meaningless, trivial, or without point. Though its meaning has proven different from what we might have expected (and perhaps from the Skeptic intention) and its truth necessary rather than established by evidence, the statement has a significance that has not yet emerged and is worth investigating. This can be brought out by looking more carefully at the term "impression" (φαντασία) as it functions in the Tropes.

Impressions are said to be *of* the object and received *from* the object.[25] In view of the difficulties surrounding the term "object" (ὑποκείμενον), the relation between impressions and both real and phenomenal objects is unclear. That the real object is the origin of impressions — the source from which we receive impressions — seems to be part of the Skeptic meaning. But what is meant by saying that impressions are *of* the object? There is a difficulty here concerning the reference of impressions, for though initially we are said to have different impressions of the "same object" and to perceive the "same objects" differently,[26] it is not the case that having an impression (of an object) is tantamount to perceiving the *real (external) object*. The point of the Tropes is to establish that having an impression does not entitle us to say anything about the real (nature of the) object. In fact the arguments seem to lead to the conclusion that to say we have different impressions of the same object does not entail that we perceive the real object at all, but that we perceive different phenomena (differ-

---

[25] *PH*, I, 40, 45, 46, 47, 52, 58, 80, 106, 124. But see also 49 where sight is said to be "receptive" (δεχόμενον) of the phenomenon.

[26] *PH*, I, 46, 47, 52, 54, 59, 124, 125, 126, 127.

ent appearances of the real object). To what objects, then, do impressions refer?

We have seen that the type of object introduced in the premise of the argument cannot be identified with either of the two types (phenomenal and real) that are found in the conclusion. There is thus an unobtrusive shift from the ambiguous and unclarified notion of an object, which enjoys the status of being both an identifiable part of someone's experience and stable in character despite its changing appearances, to the conception of a phenomenal object, of which the first of these desiderata holds but not the second, and the real object, to which the second pertains but not the first. Accordingly, we can expect between premise and conclusion an analogous displacement of the reference of impressions to either phenomenal or real objects. But it would be odd to speak of having impressions of objects that are not (recognizable or identifiable as) objects in our experience — impressions of unknowable objects. One of the implications of the Tropes is that impressions *cannot* be of the external object about which we know (can say) nothing, but can only be of phenomena. Indeed the net effect is to say that having an impression of something is a necessary and sufficient condition of perceiving it; and of course this cannot be the case, if impressions are held to be *of* external objects.[27] This implicit shift in the reference of impressions from the ambiguous notion of object to *phenomenal* object provides a suggestion for interpreting the Tropes. The argument has the effect of barring the claim that we have impressions of external objects, and by the same token it urges that our impressions (and the statements that may accompany them) refer to the phenomenal objects within experience. These considerations suggest that the Tropes may be directed against the kind of

---

[27] Sextus himself may have been aware of this consequence, for in another context (*PH*, I, 22) he speaks of the impression of a phenomenon.

philosophic theory that claims, via a doctrine of impressions, to penetrate the appearances of things to the reality that lies beyond them. The Stoic philosophy is a paradigm of such a theory.[28]

The Stoics, as we have seen, claimed that impressions can give us knowledge of the real nature of an object. But since some impressions are not accurate representations of their objects, and others may not correspond to any object at all, having an impression is not sufficient for perceiving the object. An impression must be an exact copy of its object, or we cannot be said to know the properties of that object. And this generates the problem of establishing such a relation, that is, of comparing an impression with the object it is supposed to resemble. Aenesidemus' view, on the other hand, seems to suggest that having an impression of something is necessary and sufficient for perceiving that thing, so that the problem of matching experience with its object does not arise. But in this case what the impression is *of*, and hence what is perceived, is the phenomenon and not the object underlying it. On Aenesidemus' view, we cannot say that an impression is like the external object, because the phenomenon perceived cannot be assumed to be identical with that object for the many reasons detailed in the Tropes. Therefore, we can say nothing of the character of the external object, but we can only describe its apparent properties. The force of the Tropes is most evident if they are viewed as an attack on philosophic theories (of which the Stoic is in this case perhaps the best example) that purport to transcend the data of experience to an external and, according to Skeptics, unknowable reality. The Skeptic conclusion can now be seen to have a significance that was not previously apparent. There can be no point in

[28] The Tropes are effective against any empirical doctrine that claims to unveil the real nature of things lying beyond phenomena. But the arguments are especially relevant to the Stoic (and Academic) doctrines of impressions.

affirming that we cannot know the nature of an object in principle unknowable, unless suggestion has indeed been made to the contrary. The Stoic claim that the external object is apprehended by means of impressions has, as the Skeptics very likely saw it, just that implication. Given the conditions necessary to knowing, in this case impressions, to apprehend such external realities (as distinct from phenomenal objects) is in principle impossible. Therefore, to claim knowledge of external realities is, in effect, to claim knowledge of unknowable entities.[29]

An additional passage from the text of Sextus Empiricus is helpful in establishing the relation between impression and phenomenal object.

> For Aenesidemus and his followers assert that there is a difference between phenomena, and they say that some appear to all men in common, but others to someone in particular; and of these, the ones that appear to all in common are true, but those that do not are false; whence also that which does not escape (τὸ μὴ λῆθον) common opinion (ἡ κοινὴ γνώμη) is by transferral of ἀ for μή said to be true (ἀ-ληθές).[30]

We have remarked that the relation between impression and phenomenal object is apparently such that to have an impression is to have an impression of a phenomenon, and this is equivalent to perceiving that phenomenon. Now, given the fact that two persons cannot

---

[29] Cf. the frequent references to traditional philosophers, i.e., "dogmatists": *PH*, I, 62–66, 69, 73, 85, 88, 90, 98, 128, 138, 161.

[30] *M*, VIII, 8: οἱ μὲν γὰρ περὶ τὸν Αἰνησίδημον λέγουσί τινα τῶν φαινομένων διαφοράν, καὶ φασὶ τούτων τὰ μὲν κοινῶς πᾶσι φαίνεσθαι τὰ δὲ ἰδίως τινί, ὧν ἀληθῆ μὲν εἶναι τὰ κοινῶς πᾶσι φαινόμενα ψευδῆ δὲ τὰ μὴ τοιαῦτα • ὅθεν καὶ ἀληθὲς φερονύμως εἰρῆσθαι τὸ μὴ λῆθον τὴν κοινὴν γνώμην.

Diogenes (*Vit.*, IX, 106) says more generally that the phenomenon is the criterion, according to Aenesidemus, but this is probably intended to attribute to Aenesidemus no more than the customary view of Pyrrhonists that the phenomenon is a criterion for the conduct of life.

have the same impression, that is, that an impression is not the sort of thing that can be shared,[31] the question arises whether two persons can perceive the same phenomenon. The above quotation suggests an answer to this question. Some phenomena are said to appear to all in common. The implication seems to be that even though phenomena vary according to perceptual conditions, and no two persons are in every respect alike in physical and psychic makeup, the differences that exist are not always relevant or great enough to alter significantly the character of their respective experiences. Indeed, we are told that, according to Aenesidemus, phenomena appear "virtually alike" to those in similar conditions.[32] That is, when perceptual conditions are uniform, they do not alter appreciably the content of experience, so that a phenomenal object may appear the same to more than one person (or to an individual on different occasions). If this is the meaning of "some phenomena appear to all in common," we may conclude that under uniform perceptual conditions there can be many numerically distinct impressions of the same phenomenon, which is to say, different persons in such cases will see the same phenomenal object.

The passage quoted also brings about an explicit alignment between truth and what is commonly perceived (and believed). If it can be relied upon as a correct account of Aenesidemus' view,[33] common agree-

---

[31] On the supposition that an impression is an "imprint on the mind," as the Stoics held, or at least something very similar to this.

[32] M, VIII, 215, 234: . . . τὰ δὲ φαινόμενα πᾶσι τοῖς ὁμοίως διακειμένοις παραπλησίως φαίνεται . . .

[33] The passage is apparently contradicted at M, VIII, 40, where it is implied that Aenesidemus denied that anything was true: δυνάμει δὲ καὶ ὁ Αἰνησίδημος τὰς ὁμοιοτρόπους κατὰ τὸν τόπον ἀπορίας τίθησιν. εἰ γὰρ ἔστι τι ἀληθές, ἤτοι αἰσθητόν ἐστιν ἢ νοητόν ἐστιν, ἢ καὶ νοητόν ἐστι καὶ αἰσθητόν ἐστιν. [ἢ] οὔτε δὲ αἰσθητόν ἐστιν οὔτε νοητόν ἐστιν, οὔτε τὸ συναμφότερον, ὡς παρασταθήσεται · οὐκ ἄρα ἔστι τι ἀληθές. This seems to be a serious difficulty, but it may be that the above passage is intended to be a repudiation of the true as defined in the systems Aenesidemus was attacking. The Epicureans

ment is put forth as a condition or a criterion of truth. It is not clear from the passage itself which is intended, or indeed whether the two alternatives were even distinguished by Aenesidemus. The implications of each possibility, however, are worth exploring.

The quotation might be viewed as singling out phenomena that appear to all in common as the criterion of truth.[34] Notice, however, that such an interpretation renders the passage in question incompatible with the argument in the Ten Tropes, where Aenesidemus argued, in effect, that there is no criterion of veridical experience. In that context he maintained that there is no satisfactory basis for deciding which (if any) experiences are representative of (which phenomena are identical with) their objects. And he made it abundantly clear that general agreement would not be acceptable as an "impartial" criterion. Hence, if phenomena common to all constitute, in accordance with the above quotation, a criterion of truth, Aenesidemus has flatly contradicted his position in the Ten Tropes.[35]

On the other hand, if we take the same passage at

(*M*, VIII, 9, 63) maintained that all sensibles were true and therefore existent. For there is no difference between saying that something is true and that it really exists. The Stoics (*M*, VII, 38–42; *PH*, II, 81) held that the true is intelligible and incorporeal, i.e., a proposition. Neither of these versions would be acceptable to Aenesidemus.

[34] Sextus Empiricus in a critical passage that seems without question to be directed at Aenesidemus (*M*, VIII, 53–55) interprets him in this way. He objects to the view that we can determine what is true by the number of persons in agreement about something. Cf. Chap. 5, SKEPTICISM.

[35] The contradiction (which Sextus himself does not mention), of course, does not make Sextus' interpretation, which by itself would seem to constitute strong evidence of Aenesidemus' meaning, impossible or even unlikely. But neither can we regard Sextus' interpretation of the passage as conclusive evidence of Aenesidemus' intention. Besides being a historian of philosophy, Sextus was preeminently a philosophical critic and, hence, was not always sympathetic with the views he examined. The result is that little can be said with any confidence regarding Aenesidemus' meaning. We can go no further with the present passage than to draw out its various implications.

face value, it is also plausible to suppose that common
agreement with respect to experienced phenomena is
being put forth as a (necessary and sufficient) condition
of truth. Those phenomena appearing to all in common
are perhaps being defined as true. This interpretation
does not conflict with the argument of the Ten Tropes,
for though it remains the case that there is no criterion
of veridical experience — no criterion to determine
which impressions match their objects or which phenomena are identical with real objects — the present
passage can be read as providing a different definition
of the concept of truth as it applies to phenomena, sug-
gesting a condition other than that of their established
identity with external objects. Recalling the sense statement of Timon "Honey appears sweet," we can express
this new condition under which the phenomenon of
sweetness in relation to honey is true by the translation,
"Honey appears sweet to all (or most) persons." If
honey tastes sweet to most men, then the phenomenon
appearing to these men in common is true, whereas the
individual to whom it tastes bitter must admit the
falsity of his own peculiar experience. To summarize,
though none of our impressions can be said to disclose
the real character of the world, since external objects
must be distinguished from phenomena, some phenomena appear to all in common. These can be defined
as true, in contrast with those conflicting with common
experience. General agreement with respect to experienced phenomena is the condition under which a
phenomenon is true, rather than the established coinci-
dence of phenomenon and external object.

CAUSAL EXPLANATIONS AND SIGN THEORIES

Another area of Aenesidemus' philosophical criticism
deserves attention in a study of Skeptic epistemology.
This is his critique of causal explanations (αἰτιολογίαι)
and related sign theories. The systems of traditional
philosophers were intended to supply principles ex-

planatory of phenomena, but many of these principles
or causes were inaccessible to sense, such as atoms and
the soul. These unobservable entities constituted a po-
tential source of trouble for Stoic and Epicurean philosophies, which made experience the origin of knowledge.
A theory of signs (σημεῖα) was an attempt on the part of
Stoics and Epicureans to explain how nonevident entities (ἄδηλα, ἀφανῆ), which they held to be explanatory
of observable facts, could be apprehended through the
immediately evident objects of experience (πρόδηγα,
ἐναργῆ). The effect, in many cases, was said to be a sign
of its cause. Bodily motions, for example, were interpreted by the Stoics as a sign of soul and blushing a
sign of shame.[36] A theory of signs is thus analogous to
a doctrine of evidence. It furnished a way of proceeding by inference from what is immediately given to the
unperceived. Phenomena were said to be a "vision of
the nonevident." [37] The concept of sign thereby provided for Stoics and Epicureans a crucial link between
the evident and nonevident.[38] Their claims about nonevident entities rested almost exclusively on this doctrine. Aenesidemus raised substantial objections to
existing causal explanations, and by implication to the
philosophical systems that incorporated them, and he

---

[36] *M*, VIII, 155, 173.

[37] *PH*, I, 138: ὄψις γὰρ κατ' αὐτοὺς τῶν ἀδήλων τὰ φαινόμενα. Cf.
Vit., IX, 97. There is no necessary connection between the doctrine of signs and causal explanations, but this is one way in
which the concept of sign could be very useful. Cf. Chap. 5,
SIGNS.

[38] Both Stoics and Epicureans defended a doctrine of signs, but
they disagreed over the nature of a sign. Epicureans held that it
was sensible (αἰσθητόν), and at least some of the Stoics that it was
intelligible (νοητόν) (*M*, VIII, 177, 257). According to the Epicureans, something perceived was a sign of an imperceptible cause.
For instance, motion was a sign (evident) of the void (nonevident)
(*M*, VII, 213). The Stoics claimed, on the other hand, that certain
propositions (intelligible) were signs. The perceptual proposition
"Sweat flows through the surface of the skin" is a sign (evident)
of the proposition "There exist intelligible pores" (nonevident)
(*PH*, II, 140–142; *M*, VIII, 244, 306).

accompanied his criticism with a terse rejection of the notion of sign as a basis for inference to the nonevident.

EIGHT CAUSAL TROPES. Aenesidemus' attack on philosophy proceeds by concentrating first on the allegedly explanatory character of traditional doctrines. He presents us with eight reasons for rejecting causal explanations.[39] Without singling out any specific theory for criticism, the Causal Tropes call attention to weaknesses inherent in most of the systems advanced by philosophers as explanatory of phenomenal occurrences.

1. Causal explanations as a class, inasmuch as they deal with things nonevident, derive no generally accepted support from phenomena.

2. Often, when there is a superfluity of possible causal explanations for the subject under investigation, some philosophers account for it with one explanation only.

3. To events that occur in an orderly fashion they assign causes that exhibit no order.

4. When they have grasped the manner in which phenomena occur, they think they have also apprehended how nonphenomenal entities occur, when, though it is possible that things nonevident come to pass in a manner similar to phenomena, it is also possible that they do not, but occur in a manner peculiar to themselves.

5. Practically all of them formulate causal explanations according to their own particular assumptions of fundamental principles, and not according to certain common and agreed upon methods.

6. Often they admit facts that are discovered in connection with their own assumptions, but dismiss equally credible data that conflict with these assumptions.

7. Often they assign causes that are incompatible not only with the phenomena but also with their own assumptions.

8. Often when there are equal doubts concerning the things considered apparent and the matters to be ex-

---

[39] The Tropes are quoted directly from the text of Sextus Empiricus (PH, I, 180–185).

plained, they construct theories about the doubtful, basing
them on data equally doubtful.

Commentary. The Tropes acquaint us with Aenesidemus' reasons for rejecting existing causal explanations,[40] but what is more important, together they make
up a short treatise on methodology. It is possible to discern from the above criticism a set of elementary principles to be followed in formulating philosophical
explanations. The Tropes appear to be concerned primarily with method, criteria for acceptable explanations, and the problem of the nonevident.

It is clear that Aenesidemus attributes many of the
deficiencies of causal explanations to the absence of a
standard method employed by philosophers in formulating explanations, to which 5 refers in particular.
Every doctrine has its apologists, but without established procedures none recommends itself for acceptance. The emphasis in 5 on a "common and agreed upon
method" (κοινὴ καὶ ὁμολογουμένη ἔφοδος) is worth noting
in the light of Aenesidemus' remarks concerning truth.
Here the contrast is between methods agreed upon and
practiced by all inquirers seeking to understand and
explain the same phenomena and those reflecting the
particular (ἴδιος) experience and bias of individuals.
Trope 6 suggests that the method recommended requires an impartial attention to all the facts available.
Philosophers who take into account only those phenomena that tend to confirm their own theories, while
discounting or ignoring conflicting data, display a bias
incompatible with Aenesidemus' conception of the
proper method of inquiry, as do those mentioned in 2,
who show preference for one of a number of equally
plausible explanations.

Implicit in the Tropes are some fairly general re-

---

[40] They also shed some light on Aenesidemus' conception of the
nature of causation, together with a passage (*M*, IX, 218–227) in
which he repudiates the notion of cause as a "productive"
(ποιητικός) agent.

quirements for acceptable causal explanations. It is apparent from 1 that philosophical theories that postulate nonevident entities as explanatory of phenomena are unsatisfactory, on the ground that no evidence from experience (phenomena) can be adduced in support of such unobservable entities.[41] And Aenesidemus warns in 4 against making inferences from an observed pattern of phenomenal occurrences to the nonevident. There is no reason to suppose that the regularities observed in the phenomenal world also hold of nonphenomenal objects. We need not conclude from his criticism, however, that he regarded the concept of a causal explanation as unintelligible or useless. We may suppose from 1 that he would limit explanations to the domain of phenomena. That is, phenomenal events can be explained only by reference to other observable events. Trope 3 suggests, moreover, that a causal explanation should reflect or bring out the order of phenomenal events that it purports to explain. According to 7, it ought to be consistent with the facts as well as with the assumptions of the theory of which it forms a part. Finally, such an account should be supported by experiential evidence, as suggested by 1, 2, and 8. The implication seems to be that, according to Aenesidemus, a philosophical explanation should attempt to account for phenomenal occurrences by reference to phenomena, the relations between them, and the patterns of their occurrence, rather than by invoking principles or entities that cannot be tied to experience by observational procedures.[42]

[41] By τὰ ἀφανῆ and τὰ μὴ φαινόμενα Aenesidemus seems to mean throughout the Causal Tropes, "entities unobservable in principle" rather than merely "unobserved entities." Sextus (following the Stoics) later distinguishes between different senses of "nonevident." Cf. chap. 5.

[42] Aenesidemus' criticism of causal theories for positing unobservable entities may not be consistent with his view (in the Ten Tropes of ἐποχή) that impressions are "from the object." He never explicitly refers to the external object as a "cause" (αἴτιον), but the Tropes seem to imply this.

The requirement that a philosophical doctrine be supported by evidence raises the question of what is to count as evidence, and here too the Tropes suggest no more than a general answer. Again, the notion of general agreement, this time in connection with the concept of evidence (ὁμολογουμένη ἐπιμαρτύρησις), is brought up in 1. There must be agreement that the data cited as evidence support the doctrine in question; otherwise the alleged evidence is spurious. Trope 8 implies that if there is doubt about the facts adduced or their implications, they do not qualify as evidence. That is, it is not legitimate to cite in support of a doctrine "facts" that are themselves questionable and matters of debate. As to the sort of data that will gain general acceptance, certainly the least required is that they be phenomena. But it should be noted that not even all phenomena have the capacity to bring about agreement. Some are present uniquely to one individual, whereas others are accessible to public scrutiny. The contrast in 5 between "common" and "particular" suggests that only those phenomena in principle observable by all (common to all) investigators can gain general acceptance as evidence.

Aenesidemus' criticism of causal explanations lays a general foundation for a purely empirical methodology. It signifies dissatisfaction over lack of even the most elementary agreement among philosophers concerning methods to be employed in formulating doctrines explanatory of phenomena. Without common standards adhered to by all investigators, he seems to be saying, no philosophical theory is more than conjecture.

SIGNS. It seems clear from the foregoing Tropes that philosophical theories of signs, which maintain that nonevident entities are revealed by evident data, would be unacceptable to Aenesidemus. He has repudiated as a class all causal explanations that postulate nonevident entities, on the ground that there is no evidence from experience to support them. His general position as stated in the Causal Tropes, therefore, would seem to rule out a doctrine that holds that phenomenal objects are signs or evidence of the nonevident. Accordingly, Aenesidemus has on hand an argument that specifically rejects the notion of sign as a basis for inference to the nonevident.

> If phenomena appear virtually alike to all those in a similar condition and signs are phenomena, signs appear virtually alike to all those in a similar condition; now phenomena do appear virtually alike to all those in a similar condition, but signs do not appear virtually alike to all those in a similar condition; therefore, signs are not phenomena.[43]

Commentary. The implication of the argument quoted is that phenomena cannot be regarded as evidence for nonevident entities, because it is not apparent to everyone which phenomena are signs of what. For instance, motion is a phenomenon apparent to all, but that it is a sign of something nonevident is not apparent or generally accepted. We can all agree on the fact of motion in the world, but it is not similarly apparent that motion is a sign of void, as the Epicureans claim, or a sign of soul or life, as others have urged. Aenesidemus concludes, therefore, that signs are not phenomena, hence nothing apparent is a sign of the nonevident.

His argument is equally effective against Stoic and Epicurean doctrines of signs.[44] It matters little whether the sign is conceived as sensible or intelligible. Nothing evident, whether sensible or intelligible, is a sign of the nonevident. Since both doctrines of signs are attempts to justify the introduction of nonevident en-

---

[43] *M*, VIII, 234. Cf. *M*, VIII, 215; Photius, *Bibliotheca* 170b12 (Berlin, 1824).

[44] Sextus takes this passage to be directed exclusively against the Epicureans, on the assumption that Aenesidemus is equating φαινόμενα with αἰσθητά (*M*, VIII, 216). But since the Stoics claimed that their intelligible (νοητά) signs were immediately evident (πρόδηλα), the argument is equally effective against them. Cf. *Vit.*, IX, 96–97.

tities, they violate the standards Aenesidemus has set up for philosophical inquiry. The doctrines of philosophers should attempt to explain the observed order of phenomenal occurrences without positing nonevident entities, drawing solely on phenomena as evidence to support them. Aenesidemus' criticism of causal explanations and sign theories, in conjunction with the Ten Tropes of ἐποχή, constitutes a penetrating attack on philosophic speculation.

COMPARISON WITH ACADEMIC SKEPTICISM

The recommendations suggested by Aenesidemus' critique of philosophical theories provide an interesting contrast with Carneades' criteria of truth. If Aenesidemus has provided the basis for an empirical methodology, Carneades might be said to have accomplished much the same thing. His criteria furnish a kind of method for proceeding from what might be called evidence to an assertion of fact. Still there are differences between them worth mentioning. Notably, Carneades' criteria were designed to deal with the perceptual statements of ordinary life, whereas the proposals of Aenesidemus apply to the doctrines of philosophers. Since the method implicit in Aenesidemus' criticism of causal explanations is intended to be employed in framing such theories, it is technical and would allow of more precise statement. It is in essence a rudimentary scientific method. On the other hand, the criteria of Carneades have little or nothing to do with philosophic systems. Nontechnical and resisting precise formulation, they are intended to be employed in making ordinary perceptual assertions of fact, rather than in constructing theories explanatory of those facts.

Perhaps more important in distinguishing the two philosophers is the emphasis placed by Aenesidemus on phenomena, including what may be a condition defining their truth, which gives his position a decidedly phenomenalistic cast. Neither statement nor theory should refer beyond phenomena to the nonevident, and only those phenomena appearing to all in common are true. As already noted, this excludes unobservable entities, such as atoms, soul, imperceptible pores, and the like, from the purview of philosophers. But it also rules out the real character of those objects that can be perceived. The real properties of perceptible objects themselves are nonevident, either because they are indistinguishable from the rest, or because they lie beyond phenomena and are thus inaccessible to sense. Each of the Ten Tropes led to the same conclusion, namely, we can say how an object appears to us, but we can make no statement about its real nature. In relegating the external object of sense to the class of the nonevident, Aenesidemus joins the early Pyrrhonists in denying the percipient access to the real world as opposed to its appearances. This feature of his doctrine presents the most obvious contrast with Academic Skepticism. We recall Carneades' view that even though no impression is absolutely certain (cataleptic), not all objects of perception are nonevident. An object is "seen in" (ἔμφασις) a credible impression, and the latter constitutes acceptable ground for a statement about the nature of that thing. Aenesidemus' method, on the other hand, provides a basis for a purely phenomenalistic epistemology in which the external object, deprived of any function, has become quite unnecessary.

5 * SEXTUS EMPIRICUS

Sextus Empiricus is the last major exponent of Greek Skepticism. Though the most celebrated of all the Skeptics, he is distinguished more for his contributions as a historian of philosophy than an originator of ideas. Because Sextus is the only Skeptic whose writings have survived, his unusually full and accurate accounts of the views of his predecessors constitute an indispensable source of information on classical Skepticism. On the other hand, they also reveal that his own philosophy is to a large extent the product of ideas and objectives propounded by these earlier thinkers, in particular, Pyrrho, to whom he freely acknowledges his indebtedness as a disciple, and Aenesidemus and the Empirical (Methodical) physicians, whose innovations in methodology are even more evident in his thought. But neither should the impact of the Stoics on Sextus' philosophical enterprise be overlooked. Sextus, no less than Carneades and Aenesidemus, proves to be a philosopher who must be understood against the background of Stoicism. His criticism is primarily an attack on the Stoics, and the distinctive features of his philosophy are shaped by that criticism. Nevertheless, his own doctrine is not just a mélange of earlier ideas. The influence of predecessors is manifest, but their views have been criticized, refined, and elaborated by Sextus and are frequently supplemented by ideas and arguments that cannot be traced to earlier sources. Sextus' philosophy presents us with what is perhaps the most consistent statement of an empiricist theory of knowledge in Greek philosophy. To appreciate the full measure of his skepticism, it is necessary to examine this empiricism along with his view of the nature and function of signs.

EMPIRICISM

Sextus' philosophy, like that of his Skeptic predecessors, is distinguished by its emphasis on experience as the most important factor in our knowledge of the material world. The "empiricist axiom" that knowledge originates in sensory experience receives its most explicit statement in Sextus' writings, where, at the same time, it invites more than a single interpretation.

IDEAS AND THEIR ORIGIN. Let us begin our inquiry with two quotations expressing the dependence, as Sextus sees it, of conceptual thought on sensory experience.

> Every idea, then, must be preceded by sense experience, and for this reason if sensibles are abolished, all conceptual thought is necessarily abolished along with them.[1]

The above passage implies that sense experience (αἴσθησις) is causally a necessary condition of ideas (ἐπίνοιαι) and conceptual thought (νόησις). But Sextus also holds the somewhat stronger position, that experience, as the origin of ideas, is also an important factor in determining their content.

> . . . every intelligible thing has its origin and the source of its confirmation in sense experience.[2]

Sense experience, therefore, which in some way furnishes the materials for conceptual thought, assumes a central importance in Sextus' theory of knowledge. Since this notion is not sufficiently clear in the passages

[1] *M*, VIII, 60: πάσης οὖν ἐπινοίας προηγεῖσθαι δεῖ τὴν διὰ τῆς αἰσθήσεως περίπτωσιν, καὶ διὰ τοῦτ' ἀναιρουμένων τῶν αἰσθητῶν ἐξ ἀνάγκης συναναιρεῖται πᾶσα νόησις.

[2] *M*, VIII, 356: . . . πᾶν νοητὸν τὴν ἀρχὴν ἔχει καὶ πηγὴν τῆς βεβαιώσεως ἐξ αἰσθήσεως.

cited, it will be helpful to examine Sextus' view of the nature of experience and its relation to thought in more detail.

Ideas come into being, he tells us, as a result of the encounter (περίπτωσις) or sensuous contact (θίξις) between knowing subject and the world.[3] They may result from simple sensation (an idea of white, black, sweet, or bitter), or they may be a consequence of the more complicated affair of grasping (λαμβάνειν) an object (an idea of, say, a man). Sextus here draws a distinction between what we may, for convenience, term "sensation" and "perception,"[4] which he differentiates according to both their objects and their activity or passivity.

To experience a sensation is merely to be affected sensuously in a certain manner. The subject is completely passive, and no element of judgment (concerning, for example, the reference or cause of the sensation) is present in the experience.

For these (the senses) are solely passive and are stamped like wax.[5]

When we experience a visual sensation, we are merely affected (moved) visually. To have a sensation of white is to be affected "in a whitish way" (κινεῖσθαι λευκαντικῶς, τὸ λευκαίνεσθαι) and not to apprehend that "this is white."[6] Since the senses are nonrational (ἄλογοι), they are not able to apprehend *that* something is of a certain character. Each sense, moreover, has its own proper object, so that auditory sense is aware only of sound; olfactory, of the odorous; sight, of form, size, and color. Even in the case of vision, though we sense a complex of form, size, and color, we do not sense the complex as a man or

---

[3] *M*, VIII, 56; *M*, I, 25.

[4] Sextus often uses αἴσθησις for both. He draws the distinction in terms of the presence or absence of a λογικὴ δύναμις. *M*, VII, 297; XI, 226–227.

[5] *M*, VII, 293.

[6] *M*, VII, 293–294, 344.

even a body. Sensation without the aid of mind is unable to grasp the object.[7] In short, perceiving an object
is not the same as sensing a collection of qualities. Perception involves a certain kind of mental activity (λογικὴ
δύναμις) that is capable of combining qualities so that
they are perceived as unified wholes.[8] The senses (strictly
speaking) are aware only of their objects (color, flavor,
sound), whereas in perceiving we grasp that "this is
white" or "this is sweet." [9] We also perceive that an object has different dimensions. This could not be accomplished by sensation, through which we are aware of the
surface of an object but not of the object as having
depth.[10] Perception is thus characterized by a unifying
element of judgment, which besides the ability to com-
bine ideas also involves memory. Sextus does not elaborate on the role of memory in perception, but presumably the recognition of previous similar experiences is
necessary.[11]

Going back to Sextus' account of ideas, we may conclude that ideas can be formed from anything experienced through sense, whether it be a matter of sensing
or perceiving. Sextus goes on to say that we can also
form ideas that do not correspond to anything in experience by performing certain mental operations with
experience as a base.[12] By combining ideas we conceive,
for example, of a centaur. We can also form an idea of
something resembling a component of experience.
From a likeness of Socrates we form an idea of Socrates,
though we have never seen him. Ideas can also be

---

[7] M, VII, 297–301; XI, 226.

[8] M, I, 22; VII, 297, 346; XI, 226.

[9] M, VII, 344–347. On this account it would seem that the
senses could not be charged with error, but at 345 he says:
ψεύδονταί τε ἐν πολλοῖς αἱ αἰσθήσεις καὶ διαφωνοῦσιν ἀλλήαοις. Here he
seems to be playing on the broader meaning of αἴσθησις.

[10] M, VII, 298–300.

[11] M, VII, 346. At M, VIII, 288 he speaks of a natural ability
to remember temporal sequences.

[12] For the examples that follow see M, III, 40–44; VIII, 57–61;
IX, 393–397; XI, 250–252.

framed by analogy from experience, as when in forming
an idea of the Cyclops or pygmy we begin with a conception of a man and enlarge or diminish this idea
accordingly. Fantasies, dreams, and hallucinations can
be explained in the same way. No idea, no matter how
fantastic, is completely detached from perceptual experience. Even the madman,

> . . . conceives a shape compounded of things that he has
> experienced. And in the same way one who in his sleep
> dreams of a winged man does not do so without having
> seen some winged creature and a man.[13]

On the other hand, Sextus reasons, if we had never
seen anything black (μέλαν), it would not be possible to
form an idea of it merely through the presence of something white (λευκόν).[14] We could perhaps form an idea
of black as another color — that is, a color different from
white — but it would not be an idea specifically of black.
Moreover, familiarity with an object appropriate to one
sense is not sufficient to enable us to form an idea of an
object appropriate to another sense.

> . . . for one does not by smelling something sweet arrive
> at the apprehension of white color, nor experience a sweet
> taste by perceiving the sound of a voice.[15]

IDEAS, MEANING, AND TRUTH. The examples furnished by
Sextus illustrating the relation between ideas and sensory experience all turn out to be ideas of (or directly
connected with) objects. Whether this should be attributed to chance or intention is not obvious, since he
does not expand the analysis in the direction of more
abstract concepts. Nevertheless, his own account suggests that when he speaks of an idea or conception

---

[13] *M*, VIII, 57.

[14] *M*, VIII, 209–210. The reason for this presumably is that
black (dark), being the opposite of white (light) and not com-
pounded of simpler elements, cannot be conceived in any of the
ways described above.

[15] *M*, VIII, 211.

(ἐπίνοια, νόησις), he has in mind an image. To conceive of something is to form an image of it. This interpretation is supported by several critical passages from Sextus' writings, in which he appears to assume both that an idea is an image and that its content or meaning is to be established by looking for its original in sense experience. One such criticism concerns the geometrical concept of line as length without breadth.[16] Sextus argues that we can form no idea of length without breadth and that such a conception, moreover, is internally inconsistent.

To begin with, we possess no idea of length without breadth from sensible objects. All lengths encountered in the world are perceived in conjunction with breadth, so that the geometrical notion does not arise from sense impressions. But neither can length without breadth be conceived by similarity, composition, or analogy from experience. Not through similarity, since among the objects of experience we discover nothing for the conception to resemble. But even more absurd is the suggestion that we form this idea by composition, for no data of sense can be combined so as to form a compound of length without breadth. Nor can the conception be formed analogically by way of increase or decrease, since whatever is conceived by analogy must have something in common with that from which it is conceived. But the lengths perceived in the world have nothing in common with the geometer's notion of length without breadth. Finally, it is of no avail to suppose that we form this conception by beginning with an idea of a given length having breadth and gradually diminishing the breadth until, when the latter is reduced to nothing, we ultimately end with the required notion. Though this operation can be performed, it does not achieve the desired result, since,

> . . . whenever we arrive at the point of depriving the length of its breadth altogether, we no longer conceive the

length either, but along with the removal of the breadth
the conception of the length also is removed.[17]

Because we are unable in fact to form an idea of it,
the line defined as length without breadth is therefore
inconceivable (ἀνεπινόητον).[18] Furthermore, the very concept is internally inconsistent. To attempt to form such
an idea is like trying to conceive of nonsolid body or in-
vulnerable flesh, when the very meanings of these terms
necessitate that whatever is a body is solid and that all
flesh is vulnerable. Analogously, when we conceive
length, we conceive it as including a certain breadth,
so that per impossibile to conceive length without
breadth is no longer to conceive even length.[19]

Other passages of similar bent may be found scattered
through Sextus' writings.[20] An objection against the Stoic
doctrine of lekta (and demonstration)[21] embodies similar reasoning. The Stoics maintained that, though lekta
are incorporeal, we can still receive impressions
(φαντασίαι) of them.

But they (the Stoics) also try to make their view plausible
through examples. For, they say, just as the trainer in
gymnastics or the use of arms sometimes teaches rhythms
and certain motions by taking hold of the boy's hands,
whereas at other times by standing at a distance and
moving in a certain rhythmical fashion he sets an example
for the boy to imitate, so also some objects make an im-

---

[17] M, IX, 392.

[18] Hence the idea is devoid of content (meaningless). But Sextus is too indiscriminate in his use of ἀνεπινόητον to allow us to
draw any conclusions from his use of this term concerning a
criterion of meaningfulness. He does not reserve it for ideas di-
vorced from the data of sense, but also applies it to ideas whose
meanings are not agreed upon by philosophers and to those that
engender philosophical difficulties. Cf. PH, II, 22 ff., 70, 104–
109, 118, 122–123; M, VII, 263 ff.; IX, 47.

[19] M, III, 55–57; IX, 410–412.

[20] See Sextus' criticism of the geometrical point at M, III, 23 ff.

[21] The premises and conclusions of demonstration, according
to the Stoics, are propositions (ἀξιώματα), which are incorporeal
lekta (M, VIII, 404).

print on the mind as if by touch or contact with it, as in the case of white and black bodies generally, but others are of such a nature < that as if standing at distance they set an example to be imitated>, since the mind receives an impression as a result of them but not by their agency, as in the case of incorporeal lekta.[22]

Sextus questions, however, whether we can have impressions of lekta (and hence of demonstration).

For trainers in gymnastics and the use of arms are corporeal, and accordingly they are able to produce an impression in the boy. But demonstration was set down as incorporeal, and for this reason, whether it could make an impression on the mind was questioned. The result is that the original point in question has not been established by them.[23]

He concludes, moreover, that even apart from the difficulties connected with lekta, demonstration is inconceivable. We can form no idea of demonstration, since it (or, at the very least, one of its components, namely, the conclusion) is not a part of our evident experience.[24]

The above arguments suggest very strongly that Sextus is thinking of ideas as images and that he is aware of the power of an imagist doctrine of meaning for philosophical criticism. Nevertheless, the method of tracing ideas to sense experience to determine their content, though employed effectively on numerous occasions, is not practiced consistently by Sextus. This ambivalence can be seen in passages contradicting the position stated above where, in order not to invalidate his own criticism, he feels compelled to grant that we do possess an idea of demonstration. Otherwise he is

[22] *M*, VIII, 409. There is, as indicated, apparently a lacuna in the text, restored by Kochalsky (as quoted in the Teubner edition [Mutschmann] of Sextus Empiricus).

[23] *M*, VIII, 410.

[24] *M*, VIII, 382, 386. The Stoics contended that in demonstration a nonevident conclusion is established by evident premises (*PH*, II, 140; *M*, VIII, 385).

vulnerable to the rejoinder that the Skeptic cannot undertake a critical analysis of something incomprehensible to him (something he finds inconceivable).[25] Demonstration, then, is not inconceivable, even though no such thing actually exists.

Thus far we have been able to establish that Sextus' empiricism involves both an account of the origin of ideas and what amounts to some fairly strong suggestions of an empiricist theory of meaning, which would fix the meaning or content of ideas by reference to that same sensory origin. We can fill out his position further by noting the emphasis on verifiability (confirmability) in his remarks concerning truth.

> For every statement is judged to be true or false according to its reference to the thing concerning which it is brought forward. For if it is found to be in accord with the latter, it is thought to be true, but if at variance, false.[26]

Now, Sextus continues, when that to which the statement refers is part of our evident (ἐναργές, πρόδηλον) experience, there is no difficulty in establishing that the statement is true. Thus "It is day" is confirmed by the evident fact that it is day. But when the statement refers to something inaccessible to sense (ἄδηλον, ἀποκεκρυμμένον), we are not in a position to invoke the facts either to confirm or to falsify it. For this reason statements, such as "There is void," which refer to things unobservable, are always disputed. Since they cannot be established by the facts, they must be defended by guesswork and persuasion.

> Therefore when the fact concerning which the statement is brought forth is clear and evident, it is easy for us to refer

---

[25] M, VIII, 331a: πῶς γάρ τις καὶ ζητῆσαι δύναται μηδεμίαν ἔννοιαν ἔχων τοῦ ζητουμένου πράγματος. Cf. M, VIII, 331a–337a.

It is possible, however, that Sextus is unconcerned with such inconsistencies. Elsewhere he acknowledges that his skeptical doubts apply also to his own argumentation. See notes 83 and 84; also PH, III, 280–281.

[26] M, VIII, 323.

the statement to it, and then in this fashion to say that it is true if confirmed by the fact, or false if contradicted by it. But when the fact is nonevident and hidden from us, then, since there can no longer be any secure reference of the statement to it, there remain the use of persuasive arguments and efforts to win the mind's assent from likenesses.[27]

A necessary condition of truth, according to Sextus, is verifiability in experience. And the notion of experience has, up to this point, been explicated roughly in terms of sensation and perception.

IMPRESSION AND PHENOMENON. Returning to Sextus' account of experience, we have noted that he draws a distinction analogous to that between sensation and perception. Yet he goes on to say that nothing is apprehended directly, that is, apart from the media of affections (impressions) of sense.[28] The view that all sensory experience involves receiving impressions applies equally to sensation and perception. In accordance with the earlier distinction, this means that when, in the case of sensation, we are affected "in a whitish way," sight receives an impression of white; on the other hand, when we perceive (or claim to perceive) an object, the senses variously receive impressions, which are organized by mind (impressions of a man) and to which we give our assent ("This is a man").

----

[27] *M*, VIII, 324.

[28] *M*, VII, 365: οὐδὲν δὲ ἐξ ἑαυτοῦ πέφυκε λαμβάνεσθαι ἀλλὰ πάντα ἐκ πάθους.

When expounding his own view, Sextus uses "impression" (φαντασία) almost interchangeably with "affection" (πάθος). Every impression is an affection, though the reverse might not be the case. However, as will be seen, this does not conform to the Stoic use of "impression," which is an "imprint on the mind." For the present we may say that Sextus is acknowledging a similar view of the mechanics of perception. Objects are perceived (if at all) via sense impressions (sensuous affections). The impression is produced by the object and, in the case of veridical perception, conforms to its object.

Now, Sextus continues, the external object of perception is of course not the same as an impression.[29] What is true of the one may not be true of the other (it is the fire that burns, not one's impressions of fire). Since impression and object are distinct, we are not justified in assuming uncritically that our impressions are a sure indication of the properties of the object. Upon tasting honey we cannot take the sensation of sweetness as a sign that the honey itself is sweet, since it is possible for the object in question to be capable of producing a sweet sensation without itself having that property.

> For just as the whip falling upon flesh causes pain to the flesh but is not also pain, and as the food or drink gives pleasure to the one who eats or drinks, but is not pleasure, so too fire is able to give warmth but yet not necessarily be warm, and honey to cause a sensation of sweetness but not be sweet.[30]

Moreover, impressions vary independently of any changes in the object itself. All the conditions set forth in the Ten Tropes of Aenesidemus are acknowledged by Sextus to influence the sorts of impressions received.[31] Since in every case of sensation and perception there exist conditions that affect the character of experience, there is no satisfactory way to differentiate veridical from nonveridical experience. As a consequence, we can say how an object appears but not what its real features are. Following the Pyrrhonic tradition, therefore, Sextus distinguishes between the phenomenal character of an object (φαινόμενον) and the real character over and above its appearances (ἐκτὸς ὑποκείμενον). The objects of perceptual experience are phenomena,[32] whereas the real nature of the world is unknowable.

---

[29] M, VII, 357, 365; PH, II, 72.

[30] M, VII, 368.

[31] PH, I, 36–164. Sextus fully endorses these Tropes. His exposition of them is much more elaborate than Diogenes Laertius' (Vit., IX, 79–89) and probably contains numerous examples of his own. Cf. also PH, II, 51 ff.

[32] PH, I, 9: φαινόμενα δὲ λαμβάνομεν νῦν τὰ αἰσθητά.

. . . phenomena merely establish the fact that they appear, but are not able to indicate further that they really exist (ὑπόκειται).³³

Sextus takes pains to underscore the empiricist character of his position, which, as he maintains, does not undermine the importance or reliability of sense experience as such. In fact just the opposite is the case. Never questioning the data of sense, it raises doubts only in connection with inferences drawn from phenomena.

But when we question whether the external object really is such as it appears, we grant the fact that it appears, and we do not call into question the phenomenon but what is said about the phenomenon; this is different from questioning the phenomenon itself.³⁴

We grant, he says, that honey appears sweet, because we experience a sweet sensation. The reality of experience itself is indisputable. Impressions cannot be ignored or changed at will, so their authority as a basis for action is beyond question. We cannot deny that honey tastes sweet to us or that we feel warm or cold at a given moment. In these cases assent is compelled by our own nature — by the fact that we are beings naturally capable of sensation and thought.³⁵ This is why, as he insists, the Skeptic is guided in his actions by phenomena.³⁶ Nevertheless, to affirm further that honey really is sweet is to make an inference from the undisputed datum of sense to something beyond experience — that is, to the external object.³⁷ The inference from impression (or phenomenon) to object is not compelled by nature. The fact that we are affected in a certain way, though itself undeniable, does not necessitate any conclusion about external realities.

³³ M, VIII, 368: τῶν γὰρ φαινομένων αὐτὸ μόνον παριστάντων ὅτι φαίνεται, τὸ δ' ὅτι ὑπόκειται μηκέτι προσισχυόντων διδάσκειν . . .
³⁴ PH, I, 19.
³⁵ PH, I, 13, 19, 22–24; M, VIII, 397, 203.
³⁶ PH, I, 21–25, 238.
³⁷ PH, I, 20; M, VII, 365.

Commentary. Sextus provides us with the clearest and most final explanation for the doctrine endorsed by all Pyrrhonists that assent is granted only to phenomena. Thus far we have proceeded on the supposition, based on scattered remarks in the texts, that their reasons for holding this view are both theoretical and practical — theoretical because acquaintance with phenomena does not warrant beliefs or assertions about external objects, and practical because the Skeptic, though he suspends judgment with respect to the reality of things, requires a standard (phenomenon) on which to act. Sextus' reasoning constitutes an endorsement of that view. There is no justification for beliefs about objects, since such beliefs are inferential, based on impressions that are distinct from the objects themselves and whose character need not be representative of objects. To take one's own condition as revealing the nature of the external world is to confuse the impression of an object with the object itself. Sextus' remarks, moreover, add a further reason for granting assent to phenomena. If the Pyrrhonist is asked why he bases his actions on phenomena rather than something else, or why he concedes that assent even to phenomena is justified, he may reply (following Sextus) by giving what appears to be an essentially psychological explanation, namely, that assent to our own impressions is compelled by our nature as creatures "naturally capable of sensation and thought."[38] Postponing consideration of the role of thought in this natural process, let us note first the close connection in Sextus' account between having impressions and granting assent to phenomena.

Sextus' example acknowledging that honey appears sweet, regardless of its real properties, brings to mind the almost identical assertion of Timon, from which we were led originally to draw a comparison between sense statements and perceptual statements. The contrast is

---

[38] *PH*, I, 24: . . . ὑφηγήσει μὲν φυσικῇ, καθ' ἣν φυσικῶς αἰσθητικοὶ καὶ νοητικοί ἐσμεν . . .

especially illuminating in relation to Sextus' doctrine, for it allows us to catalog very nicely all the distinctions he takes to be significant.

First, it marks the contrast between phenomenon and external object. A sense statement makes a claim, not about what exists independently of perceptual conditions, but only about the object as it forms a part of experience. Perceptual statements, on the other hand, refer to objects that are not, or cannot be identified as, objects of experience. Also relevant is the distinction between sense impression and object. Impressions cannot be identified with the objects from which they arise. Since impressions vary independently of the object, we are able to describe our impressions (sense statement) but not the real features of the object (perceptual statement). Finally, we return to Sextus' initial distinction between sensation and perception. The contrast between sense statements and perceptual statements fits well here. In sensation we are merely affected sensuously without referring the experience to any reality distinct from it. Perception, however, entails a judgment about the external object ("Honey is sweet," "This is a man"). The two types of statement suggest a very close relationship, on the one hand, between sensation, impression, and phenomenon, and, on the other, between perception and external object. The suggestion is revealing, for though (from Sextus' account thus far) it looks as if we are dealing with three sorts of entity (impression, phenomenon, and object), this turns out not to be the case. Sextus, in an apparently offhand manner, identifies impression and phenomenon.

> As for the criterion of the Skeptic movement, therefore, we say that it is the phenomenon, applying this term to what is, in effect, the impression of it; for since our impressions depend on the fact of our own susceptibility, that is, on our being affected independently of our will, they are not open to question. Hence no one, I suppose, disputes that the underlying object appears this way or that, but the

matter in question is whether it really has the character it appears to have.[39]

The final reason, therefore, why assent is granted to phenomena is that phenomena are identical with impressions to which assent is compelled by nature.

Consider the consequences of Sextus' identification of phenomenon and impression for the sensation-perception dichotomy. If his contention that both sensation and perception occur through the agency of impressions tends to blur this distinction, his identification of impression and phenomenon obliterates it completely. For, strictly speaking, impressions are only sensuous affections.[40] We can see this clearly from Sextus' own example. The reason why we grant that honey appears sweet, he says, is that "we experience a sweet sensation" (γλυκαζόμεθα γὰρ αἰσθητικῶς).[41] Now it would seem to follow from the identification of impression and phenomenon that to say honey appears sweet is to describe the impressions one is having — that is, to describe one's sensations. Sextus' position therefore ends by reducing all sensory experience to a species of sensation. There is no such thing as perception. In cases alleged to be perceiving, what is actually given to sense and subsequently grasped is the phenomenon, and this, as it turns out, is *not* the object but only the impressions (sensations) experienced by a percipient. The object itself is not in any sense a part of experience. There is of course an existing

[39] By "criterion" Sextus does not mean a criterion of truth, but a criterion for the conduct of life. *PH*, I, 22: κριτήριον τοίνυν φαμὲν εἶναι τῆς σκεπτικῆς ἀγωγῆς τὸ φαινόμενον, δυνάμει τὴν φαντασίαν αὐτοῦ οὕτω καλοῦντες · ἐν πείσει γὰρ καὶ ἀβουλήτῳ πάθει κειμένη ἀζήτητός ἐστιν. διὸ περὶ μὲν τοῦ φαίνεσθαι τοῖον ἢ τοῖον τὸ ὑποκείμενον οὐδεὶς ἴσως ἀμφισβητεῖ, περὶ δὲ τοῦ εἰ τοιοῦτόν ἐστιν ὁποῖον φαίνεται ζητεῖται.

[40] This is a departure from the Stoic notion of impression. On Sextus' view it is impossible to have an impression that this thing is white or sweet, or even, for that matter, an impression that this thing appears white or sweet. See below.

[41] *PH*, I, 20.

object (ἐκτὸς ὑποκείμενον), but it is never perceived. Experience consists of impressions, and these are also the *objects* of experience.

Nevertheless, there seems to be a difficulty in holding both that sensation, unlike perception, involves no mental activity, being no more than the passive affection of the sense organ by its proper object; and at the same time, what seems to be implied by the assimilation of phenomenon to impression, that to assert that honey appears sweet, for example, is merely to describe one's impressions or sensations. For the transition from the passive awareness that is experiencing a sweet taste sensation to the assertion that honey tastes sweet presupposes a unifying mental activity of the sort that Sextus elsewhere attributes only to perception. That is, to say that honey *appears* sweet implies that a certain aggregate of sensations has been unified and recognized as honey, just as is the case when we assert that honey *is* sweet. If sense statements are descriptive of impressions, then to be able to describe one's impressions in such an assertion implies a mental activity over and above the process of sensing itself, which, as Sextus tells us, is a nonrational occurrence. The crucial difference between assenting to a perceptual statement (descriptive of the object) and assenting to a sense statement (descriptive of impressions) is not, therefore, the presence of a mental activity in the one and its absence in the other. (This is indicated by Sextus' remark that the natural capacity for sensation *and thought* compels us to assent to our impressions.) The distinguishing feature of assent to impressions (sensations) is the necessity (ἠναγκασμένα πάθη) that compels acceptance independently of any reflection or deliberation (ἀβουλήτως). On the other hand, we are free to give or withhold assent to assertions about the real properties of an object, not being compelled by nature to hold any beliefs about external objects.

We have yet to explore Sextus' reasons for identifying

phenomena with impressions.⁴² As already noted, that step seems a departure from his original position that having impressions is necessary for perceiving an object. From there he argued that since impressions vary independently of their objects, the phenomenal object cannot be (said to be) identical with the external object. But his argument, of course, does not entail that phenomenon is identical with impressions (that the object of experience is the same as our impressions of it). To say that we apprehend objects via impressions is not the same as saying that we apprehend impressions. Sextus gives no explanation for this equation, but the basis for it may not be difficult to discern. For if it is the case, as he claims, that our experiences (impressions) vary according to diverse perceptual conditions, it would be tempting for him to conclude (following Aenesidemus) that what is perceived (phenomenon) varies in an identical fashion. That is, what I see when I judge an object to be white is something different from what you see when you say it is yellow. And since phenomena are among the things that vary with the conditions of perception, they are, in this important respect, like impressions and unlike objects. What is perceived, therefore, may be nothing but the impressions (affections) received from the external object. Whether or not this exactly reproduces Sextus' reasoning is of course uncertain, but his position that impressions are the objects of sensory experience is clear.

> . . . and the senses do not grasp external objects, but only, if anything, their own affections.⁴³

As for the original contention that impressions are the media of perception, that seems to be part of his

---

⁴² The important equation is between "phenomenon," on the one hand, and "impression," "affection," or "sensation," on the other, since the last three terms are all very close in meaning.

⁴³ PH, II, 72. Cf. M, VII, 300, 354. The qualification "if anything" marks Sextus' unwillingness to assert that, strictly speaking, the senses know or "grasp" (καταλαμβάνειν) anything.

strategy of attack against the Stoic theory, in which impressions played an important part. Granting the premise of impressions and their necessary role in perception, Sextus can show that objects can never be perceived.

The Stoics held that an impression was an imprint on (alteration of) the mind, produced by an object and representative of that object. Sextus was quick to see weaknesses in that view. He pointed out, as the Stoics themselves maintained, that the intellect does not receive impressions directly from the object but only by way of sense. And affections of sense are not to be confused with the object from which they arise. If, therefore, an impression is an imprint on the mind, it will not be of the external object, on the Stoic account, but only of the affections of sense.

> . . . and the impressions, then, will be of the affections of sense, which are different from the external object; for honey is not the same as my sensation of sweetness nor wormwood the same as my sensation of bitterness, but a different thing.[44]

Moreover, it will not do to argue that we can perceive objects because of their similarity to affections (sensations). How can we compare our sensations with objects to establish their similarity, when we have never encountered these entities in experience?

> For just as a man who does not know Socrates, but has seen a picture of him, does not know whether the picture is like Socrates, so too the mind, when it looks upon the affections of sense but does not contemplate the external objects, will not know whether the affections of sense are like the objects.[45]

The Stoic theory, therefore, does not establish that we perceive objects, or even that we have impressions of

[44] PH, II, 72. Cf. M, VII, 354, 381–384.
[45] PH, II, 75. Cf. M, VII, 357–358, 367–368, 384–385. This is perhaps Sextus' most important argument against the Stoic cri-

objects. Though Sextus is willing for his own purposes
to retain the term "impression," on his account impressions are not distinct from sensuous affections. Not a
means for perceiving external objects, they are themselves the objects of experience.

Consider Sextus' conception of phenomenon in contrast with the view of Aenesidemus. Though phenomena are for both the objects of perception, Sextus'
identification of impression and phenomenon marks a
significant difference between them. Following Aenesidemus, we may say that having an impression is necessary and sufficient for perceiving a phenomenon, but the
impression is not identical with the phenomenon perceived. An impression is an affection of the subject,
whereas the phenomenon is the object as it is perceived.
On Sextus' account, however, the object drops out completely as the reference of impressions. Impressions are
received from the external object, but they cannot be
of that object. Nor can they be *of* the phenomenal object, for impression and phenomenon are identical. It
follows, therefore, that we do not perceive the object
in any form, but only our own impressions. A consequence of the view that impressions are what is seen,
heard, tasted, and the like, is that there is a separate
impression, in the case of vision, for example, corresponding to every instance of seeing, since presumably
impressions are numerically distinct, if not always distinguishable in other respects. From the identification
of impression and phenomenon we can conclude that
the object seen is also different (at least numerically) in
every case of visual experience. The result is that what
is ordinarily taken to be a case of seeing the same object
on different occasions or from different points of view
is, on Sextus' account, not seeing the same thing but
seeing numerous similar (perhaps indistinguishable)
but, nevertheless, distinct impressions. Strictly speaking,

---

terion of truth (cataleptic impression). For other objections see
PH, II, 70–80; *M*, VII, 370–440.

it would be incorrect to say we ever see, hear, touch the same thing. A proper name or a definite description must stand for an indefinite number of phenomena (impressions), viewed by countless persons on occasions and under circumstances of an untold number and variety. Sextus' philosophy, therefore, ends in an extreme form of empiricism. The data of experience are sensations (impressions), which are private to the subject and furnish no information about the external world. The percipient is aware only of his impressions, which are original in every case of sensory experience.

SIGNS

We are able to gain additional insight into Sextus' theory of knowledge by studying his criticism of the Stoic theory of signs.[46] This aspect of Stoic epistemology is the basis for the claim that knowledge of unperceivable entities is possible. The theory rests on the distinction between the (immediately) evident (πρόδηλον, ἐναργές) and the nonevident (ἄδηλον). Anything evident to sense or mind is grasped by a cataleptic impression. But the sign makes inferences about the nonevident possible when they are based on immediately evident data. Following is a brief exposition of the Stoic doctrine.[47]

STOIC THEORY OF SIGNS. All existing things, according to the Stoics, can be classified as either (immediately) evident or nonevident (though the two classes are not mutually exclusive). The evident includes all those things immediately present to sense or mind. Whatever can be known through itself alone (whatever is grasped by a cataleptic impression) and requires no further evidence to establish it, is immediately evident. For exam-

---

[46] Though Sextus' criticism also extends to the Epicurean doctrine that signs are sensible objects, for the sake of brevity and to avoid repetition, this account concentrates on the Stoic theory.

[47] The following account of Stoic doctrine is taken from PH, II, 97 ff.; M, VII, 358, 364–365; M, VIII, 141 ff., 316 ff.

ple, the fact at the present moment that it is day or that this is a man, and the corresponding perceptual propositions, are evident. The nonevident, on the other hand, includes whatever is not immediately given in this fashion, so that, if known at all, it is known by inference from the evident. The Stoics divided the nonevident into three classes: absolutely (καθάπαξ) nonevident, naturally (φύσει) nonevident, and temporarily (πρὸς καιρόν) nonevident. Things falling into the third class, though perfectly evident in themselves, at times are rendered nonevident owing to contingencies, such as distance or time. Hence, Sextus says the city of Athens is temporarily nonevident to him. What is temporarily nonevident is so only in relation to a given subject and may at the same time be immediately evident to others. The naturally nonevident, on the other hand, comprises those things by nature hidden from our apprehension, but for which there is evidence from what is immediately evident. The contentions of philosophers that there are imperceptible pores in the skin or indivisible elements moving in a void concern naturally nonevident entities. Absolutely nonevident, however, are those things for which there is no evidence one way or the other, for example, whether the stars are even or odd in number or that there are so many grains of sand in Libya.[48] Of these four classes of things, the Stoics maintained, as already noted, that the immediately evident is made up of entities (facts) known of themselves and without further evidence, whereas the absolutely nonevident contains entities that cannot be known at all. Things temporarily and naturally nonevident, however, can be known indirectly, that is, by means of signs, which constitute evidence for their existence or truth.

Generally speaking, Sextus tells us, a sign is that which is thought to reveal something — more specifi-

---

[48] At *M*, VIII, 317–320 Sextus calls the latter class naturally nonevident instead of absolutely nonevident. But this goes against his account at *M*, VIII, 145 ff., and *PH*, II, 97 ff.

cally, to reveal a nonevident object. The Stoics held that signs must be immediately evident to be able to reveal (signify) something nonevident.[49] Just as there are two sorts of nonevident entity revealed by signs, there are two corresponding types of sign in Stoic epistemology. The associative sign (τὸ ὑπομνηστικὸν σημεῖον) signifies something temporarily nonevident, and the indicative sign (τὸ ἐνδεικτικὸν σημεῖον) something naturally nonevident.

The associative sign, having been observed frequently in conjunction with the object signified, calls to mind the object previously observed along with it, when the latter is temporarily nonevident. For example, smoke has frequently been observed in conjunction with fire, so that the presence of smoke calls fire to mind, even though the thing signified is not at the moment visible. By the same process of association past and future events are suggested. On seeing a scar, we recall the wound that preceded it, and we associate a puncture of the heart with impending death. The indicative sign, on the other hand, does not admit of being observed in conjunction with the object signified. Nevertheless, the Stoics claimed, it reveals "of its own nature and constitution, speaking out with its own voice" a naturally nonevident object.[50] Thus, the soul is revealed by the motions of the body, for we reason that there is a certain power within the body which causes these motions.

Thus far it may seem as if the Stoics are merely giving a description of psychological fact — that is, what might be regarded as a natural capacity and tendency to associate ideas and draw inferences. But the theory of signs is more than a descriptive account of a psychological process. It is a doctrine, incorporated by the Stoics into the framework of their deductive logic, which attempts to justify such inferences. A sign (associative and indicative) was taken to be sufficient evidence for an inference

[49] M, VIII, 143, 173.
[50] M, VIII, 154.

about the nonevident. The Stoics defined the sign as a true antecedent proposition in a true conditional, capable of revealing the consequent.[51] For example, the proposition "There is smoke" is a sign (associative) revealing a temporarily nonevident consequent, for it is a true antecedent in the true conditional "If there is smoke, then there is fire." Similarly, "Bodily motions exist" is an indicative sign of the proposition "Soul exists," because as antecedent in the resultant true conditional, it reveals a naturally nonevident consequent. These true conditionals (sign and nonevident consequent) were then employed as premises in valid arguments of the form: If A, then B; A; therefore, B. The theory of signs thus enabled the Stoics to establish a nonevident conclusion in a valid deductive argument.

As might be expected, Sextus' criticism of the Stoic theory is directed almost exclusively against the indicative sign. He has no argument with the associative sign and even adopts as his own view a version of that part of the doctrine of signs. Let us first examine his critique of the indicative sign[52] and then consider his remarks concerning the associative sign.

CRITIQUE OF THE INDICATIVE SIGN. Sextus' account of sense experience, as determined thus far, has the effect of

----

[51] *M*, VIII, 245: ὑπογράφοντες τοίνυν φασὶ σημεῖον εἶναι ἀξίωμα ἐν ὑγιεῖ συνημμένῳ καθηγούμενον, ἐκκαλυπτικὸν τοῦ λήγοντος. *M*, VIII, 250: τοίνυν ὅταν λέγηται τὸ σημεῖον ἀξίωμα εἶναι ἐν ὑγιεῖ συνημμένῳ καθηγούμενον, δεήσει ἐν μόνῳ ἀκούειν αὐτὸ καθηγούμενον συνημμένῳ τῷ ἀπ' ἀληθοῦς τε ἀρχομένῳ καὶ ἐπ' ἀληθὲς λήγοντι. Cf. *PH*, II, 104–107.

When discussing signs, Sextus does not always treat them as propositions, for example, when he says that some signs are, and others are not, observed along with (συμπαρατηρεῖσθαι) the thing signified (*PH*, II, 100; *M*, VIII, 152, 154). This is probably explained by the fact that the Epicureans, unlike the Stoics, maintained that signs were sensibles (hence observable). And Sextus himself held that some phenomena are signs. Though the Stoic sign (proposition) is not the sort of thing that can be observed, it was nevertheless said to be immediately evident.

[52] Only those arguments against the indicative sign that help to uncover Sextus' own epistemology are presented here.

neutralizing the distinction between evident and non-evident, as defined by the Stoics, and thus undermining their doctrine of signs, which is based on that distinction. Since all perceptual objects, both evident and non-evident (according to the Stoic definition), ultimately must be grasped (if at all) through the media of impressions (affections), and (as Sextus has argued) we cannot justifiably claim that our impressions reveal the nature of the external object, all such objects are nonevident.[53] It follows that perceptual propositions (and statements), which refer to such realities, are also nonevident. That is, propositions, such as "There is smoke" and "Bodily motions exist" cannot be signs of the nonevident, since they (and the entities to which they refer) are themselves nonevident, whereas a sign was said by the Stoics to be something immediately evident. Sextus' own view of experience, therefore, blocks the notion of sign as an evident perceptual proposition, by ruling out the possibility that perceptual propositions as such, none of which refer to the phenomenal objects of experience, can be evident.[54] Sextus is aware of this consequence,[55] but he has independent arguments to bring against the Stoic theory of signs.

Even if we grant that a perceptual proposition is evident, it cannot reveal something naturally nonevident. That is to say, no perceptual proposition is an indicative sign, for if it were capable by its very nature of indicating a nonevident consequent, it would be indicative of the same thing to everyone.[56] Yet in the case of

[53] *M*, VII, 358, 364–367.

[54] In the present context perceptual propositions ("X really is Y") cannot be evident signs, because they refer to nonphenomenal entities. But Sextus also has more fundamental objections to the notion of proposition (and lekton in general) as an incorporeal entity. Cf., *M*, VIII, 70, 75, 79, 85–86, 261, 410; *PH*, II, 107–110.

[55] *M*, VIII, 141–142.

[56] *M*, VIII, 189, 201, 274, 322. The argument at 189 is against the Epicurean sign, but the same reasoning applies to the Stoic theory.

signs there is not always agreement as to what is signified by them. If, for example, a man's fall from wealth
to poverty is said by one to be a sign of extravagant
living, by another a sign of disaster by sea, and by a
third a sign of his generosity to friends, we cannot say
that the event by its very nature signifies any one of
these things. Analogously, the fact that indicative signs
do not lead everyone to the same conclusions demonstrates that by themselves they do not reveal anything.
Not everyone agrees that the existence of soul is indicated by bodily motions or that blushing is a sign of
shame. Disputes over what is signified by an indicative
sign are an inevitable result of the inaccessibility of
those facts or entities.[57] Disagreements in such cases
cannot be settled. Consequently, even though it be
granted that an object (or proposition) is evident, the
claim that it is a sign of something nonevident is itself
nonevident.[58] No one would call into question the
proposition "Bodily motions exist" (granted by hypothesis to be evident), but that it is indicative of the
nonevident proposition "Soul exists" is a matter of
doubt. Since the consequent makes a claim that cannot
be established by experience, it is a fortiori not established by the indicative sign. It is false, then, to say
that the antecedent (sign) reveals or constitutes conclusive evidence of the consequent. Disagreements over
what is signified by the indicative sign demonstrate
that it provides no evidence at all. Conflicting opinions
in regard to what nonevident facts appear to be signified by evident experience can be explained by our
varying dispositions and experiences.[59]

This points to a significant difference, Sextus tells
us, between indicative and associative signs. The effectiveness of the associative sign is not similarly destroyed

---

[57] *PH*, II, 116; *M*, VIII, 265–269, 332–334.

[58] This is an expanded version of Aenesidemus' argument
against signs. Cf. *M*, VIII, 215, 234.

[59] *M*, VIII, 197. Here again the argument is directed specifically
against the "sensible" sign.

by differing opinions as to what is signified by it. Since
associative signs are sometimes established by convention, they may be expected to signify different things to
different persons. The raising of a torch may announce
to some the approach of enemies, but to others the ar-
rival of friends. The sound of a bell signifies the selling
of meat to some and to others the need to water the
roads. Signs established by convention can be made to
indicate one thing or many depending on our wishes
and needs.

> For they are determined, as they say, by the lawgivers and
> are in our power, whether we wish them to make known
> one thing or to be significative of many.[60]

The indicative sign, on the other hand, is supposed to
reveal something of its own nature (ἐκ φύσεως). Since the
power of signifying is held to be in the object itself, and
we are therefore not in a position to establish its significance, the indicative sign should signify the same
thing to everyone. The fact that it does not casts doubt
on the notion that evident objects can have an intrinsic
capacity to reveal the nonevident.

Addressing the Stoics in their own terms, Sextus
argues that since the sign is defined as a true antecedent
proposition in a true conditional, capable of revealing
the consequent, no antecedent proposition can be
claimed for an indicative sign, because the truth of the
conditional itself in such a case cannot be established.
Take the proposition, "If sweat flows through the surface, the skin has intelligible pores." The antecedent is
said to be an indicative sign. Now the truth of that
proposition may be granted, but a conditional with true
antecedent is true only if the consequent is true. In the
above example, however, the consequent is by hypothesis naturally nonevident, so that its truth cannot be
established. Therefore the truth (or falsity) of the con-

[60] M, VIII, 200.

ditional itself cannot be decided (ἀνεπίκριτον).⁶¹ Sextus concludes, therefore, that nothing is an indicative sign, because no naturally nonevident proposition (or statement) can be confirmed or falsified.

> Accordingly, the Skeptics very neatly compare those who inquire about nonevident things to those who are shooting at a mark in the dark; for just as it is likely that one of them hits the mark whereas another misses, but who has hit or missed cannot be known, so too when the truth is hidden almost in the depths of darkness, though many statements are cast out at it, which of these are in accord with it and which at variance cannot be known, since the object of inquiry is fixed beyond the sphere of the evident.⁶²

He goes on to show that the Stoic attempt to incorporate the indicative sign into their system of logic, in order to bestow on knowledge claims the certainty of deductive inferences, is likewise a failure. For if an argument (of the form, if A, then B; A; therefore, B) is said to demonstrate a nonevident conclusion B with the help of an indicative sign A, the conditional proposition that forms one of its premises will also be nonevident. And there is no more justification for assuming the truth of a nonevident premise than for assuming the truth of the conclusion itself.

> . . . if the assumption, insofar as it is assumed, is certain and sure, let the dogmatic philosophers assume not the things from which they deduce the nonevident but the nonevident itself, that is, not the premises of the demonstration but the conclusion.⁶³

Consequently, a valid argument, if it contains an indicative sign in one of its premises, is not demonstrative,

⁶¹ *M*, VIII, 267–268, 334. 268: τὸ οὖν περιεκτικὸν τοῦ τε σημείου καὶ τοῦ σημειωτοῦ συνημμένον, λῆγον ἐπὶ ἄδηλον, ἐξ ἀνάγκης ἐστὶν ἀνεπίκριτον.

⁶² *M*, VIII, 325.

⁶³ *M*, VIII, 374. Cf. *PH*, I, 174.

because it cannot establish a nonevident conclusion.[64] Take, for example, the argument, "If sweat flows through the surface, the skin has intelligible pores; sweat flows through the surface; therefore, the skin has intelligible pores." Through valid, it does not demonstrate the nonevident conclusion, since the truth of the conditional proposition, the premise containing the indicative sign, is in doubt.

ASSOCIATIVE SIGN. Sextus' objections to the indicative sign focus on the naturally nonevident consequent it was held to disclose. His criticism does not extend to the associative sign, which, according to the Stoics, has a consequent that is temporarily nonevident. It is this feature of the associative sign that makes it broadly acceptable to Sextus. He does not, of course, endorse the Stoic notion of sign as an (evident) proposition, but his own view of the associative sign as phenomenon comes very close to an acceptance of that part of the Stoic theory. Phenomena, for Sextus, can be related as sign and thing signified. Objects signified by the associative sign, owing to some contingency or other, are not within our sensory field, but they are entities that can be, and have been, perceived by us.

> As it is, then, since we affirm the associative sign, which ordinary persons employ, but abolish the sign falsely imagined by the dogmatists, besides not ever coming into conflict with ordinary life, we even act as its advocates, inasmuch as we refute the dogmatists, who have risen up against common preconception and declared that they know things naturally nonevident from inquiring into nature by means of signs.[65]

Sextus' reasons for adopting the associative sign concern the existence of an observable relation between sign

[64] *M*, VIII, 334, 451–452. The Stoics defined demonstration as a valid argument with true premises that reveal a nonevident conclusion (*PH*, II, 143; *M*, VIII, 310; *Vit.*, VII, 45).

[65] *M*, VIII, 158. Cf. *PH*, II, 102, 246, 254.

and thing signified. That is, there is reason for asserting that an evident object is a sign of something temporarily nonevident, if the two have frequently been observed to occur together.[66] We are naturally capable of remembering past experiences and their temporal sequences, so that because we remember that smoke and fire have occurred together in the past, in accordance with a "theoretical art" (θεωρητικὴ τέχνη) that deals with phenomena, we take the phenomenon of smoke to be a sign of fire when the fire cannot at the moment be seen.[67] By the same natural ability to remember and associate phenomena we infer past and future events, employing general rules or principles (θεωρήματα) arrived at by numerous observations. We can foretell (προγιγνώσκειν) death from a puncture of the heart and infer a previous wound from an evident scar. The sorts of phenomena mentioned have frequently been observed to occur in temporal sequence and are thus mentally associated in the same order. In each case the sign is evident and the thing signified temporarily nonevident. If such sequences were not observed (or remembered), we would have no reason to suppose that a pair of events are related as sign and thing signified. This explains the failure of the indicative sign in Sextus' estimation as well as his endorsement of the associative sign.

Commentary. The above exposition raises some interesting questions about Sextus' view of the nature and function of signs. It is clear that he regards the associative sign as a basis for inference about phenomena past, present, and future. He stresses the observable character of the kinds of phenomena so related and our natural capacity to remember and associate past experiences. He thus seems to consider inferences of this sort both natural, in the sense that they are no more than normal psychological processes, and justified because of their empirical ground. We can explore this last notion some-

---

[66] *M*, VIII, 152–154; *PH*, II, 100, 102.
[67] *M*, VIII, 288, 291.

what further by looking at Sextus' remarks about signs together with some comments he makes in other contexts.

Two relevant characteristics of sign and thing signified can be elicited from the passages specifically concerned with signs. First, the objects (or types of objects) so related are observable, even though in a particular instance the one is temporarily nonevident; and second, these (types of) objects have been observed to occur together or in a particular sequence on many previous occasions. Neither feature belongs to the indicative sign, which Sextus rejects, and it is not unlikely that he would regard both as conditions necessary for any two entities to be related as sign and thing signified. Closely connected with the observable and repeatable character of these phenomena is the fact that a connection of the sort Sextus finds acceptable, if it is alleged to hold between two phenomena, can in most cases be confirmed (or disconfirmed). That is, we can look for the fire that is expected to accompany smoke, inquire of the scarred individual concerning his previous wound, and observe the man die whose heart has been punctured. This consideration is no doubt important to Sextus, for in the passages on truth he emphasizes the necessity that statements be verifiable by evident empirical facts to be called true.[68] No statement affirming that one thing is a sign of another, therefore, can be said to be true, unless such a relation has been and can continue to be, established in experience.

Sextus' comments on signs also contain the notion of a particular art or discipline that concerns itself with phenomena. Essential to this discipline, he tells us, are general principles (θεωρήματα) issuing out of repeated observations of phenomena.[69] These remarks coincide with what he has to say in another context, in which he is critical of the astrologers.

---

[68] *M*, VIII, 323–326.
[69] *M*, VIII, 291: διὰ γὰρ τῶν πολλάκις τετηρημένων ἢ ἱστορημένων ποιεῖται τὰς τῶν θεωρημάτων συστάσεις.

And just as in medicine we have observed that a puncture of the heart is the cause of death, after observing along with it not only the end of Dion but also of Theon and Socrates and many others, so too in astrology if it is credible that this particular configuration of stars is significative of a certain kind of life, then by no means has it been observed only once in a single case but many times in many cases.[70]

The quoted passage reinforces the idea that general statements explanatory of phenomena are formulated only after repeated observations of particular instances. And in the same context he affirms that these generalizations form a basis for prediction (πρόρρησις), which is not reliable unless based on many observations.[71] Consequently, we can suppose that in the discussion of signs, when Sextus speaks of knowing in advance (προγιγνώσκειν) certain events, he is thinking of the predictive power of general statements descriptive of a large number of phenomenal occurrences. Such phenomena can be said to be related as sign and thing signified, when they have repeatedly been observed to occur together or in a particular temporal relation.

Sextus' rejection of the indicative sign amounts to a denial that the concept of sign is applicable in cases involving unobservable entities. Thus his argument with the Stoics ultimately reduces to a controversy over the nature of evidence. To deny that phenomenal entities are signs of the nonevident entails the denial of empirical evidence for the existence of nonevident entities. The reason for Sextus' stance is that no phenomenon can be observed to occur in any relation whatever to a nonphenomenal object. Consequently, without such an observational base it is impossible to establish any repeated pattern of occurrence to be used as a basis for reliable predictions in similar but unobserved cases. The outcome of his reasoning is a sharpening of the

[70] *M*, V, 104.
[71] *M*, V, 103. Cf. also *M*, V, 2.

concept of sign or evidence. No object in experience is intrinsically suggestive of anything else. To claim one object as evidence for another is not to detect and describe a property of that object, namely, that of being a sign of the other, but to affirm an observable relation between them — a relation established by previous observation of the behavior of numerous entities of the same sort. If such a relation has not been determined consistently to hold between two types of phenomenon, there is no justification for maintaining that one is a sign of the other and thus drawing inferences from the one to the other. The justification for inferences to the unknown is grounded not in the dubious apprehension of an "indicative" property belonging to an object or to objects of a certain sort, but in the consistency of a pattern of occurrence observed to hold in respect of two types of phenomenon. Consequently, the relation of "being a sign of" (or "being evidence for") is applicable only to pairs of entities (1) that are in principle observable and (2) that have in fact been observed to occur together or in a particular relation on many occasions. Sextus' argument completely removes the concept of sign or evidence from the domain of unobservable entities.

SKEPTICISM

Sextus' endorsement of the associative sign presupposes the use of inductive inferences throughout. We might expect, therefore, that he would acknowledge induction as a reliable method of arriving at conclusions about the nonevident. Further, his remarks on truth and the emphasis placed on verifiability suggest that sense statements, which are limited to a description of phenomena, and which therefore can be confirmed or falsified in experience, are true or false. Nevertheless, Sextus contradicts both of these expectations. In a passage specifically devoted to induction, he denies the validity of inductive inferences and, on more than one occasion, declares that nothing whatever is true.

INDUCTION. The following passage criticizes the notion of induction (ἐπαγωγή) generally as a form of inference.

> And I think the method of induction is also easily disposed of. For when through its means they profess to establish the universal from the particulars, they will accomplish this by reviewing either all the particulars or some. But if they review some, the induction will be uncertain, since it is possible that some of the particulars left out in the induction will contradict the universal; and if all, they will be laboring at the impossible, since the particulars are countless and unlimited. Thus it follows on either side, I think, that induction is shaky.[72]

Commentary. Sextus' comments on induction are puzzling, because they seem to conflict with his endorsement of the associative sign. This difficulty can be resolved, however, by looking at the context in which his criticism of induction occurs and also by recalling his statements about truth. The passage quoted appears in the midst of a discussion of deductive arguments (συλλογισμοί). In the pages immediately preceding the quotation, Sextus points out the absurdity of arguments that make use of a universal statement as premise, having established that premise inductively, in order to deduce particular statements from it. The reasoning is circular, since the logicians establish the universal statement by means of the particulars and then proceed to deduce logically the particular statements from the universal.[73] It is likely that the passage quoted above, since it follows immediately upon this criticism of deductive arguments for their circularity, is also intended to point out a weakness of inductive reasoning when it is employed in deductive arguments. That is, if we propose to establish the truth of the premise(s) inductively, then since the induction will always be uncertain (ἀβέβαιος), the conclusion, though deduced logically from the premise(s), will also be uncertain.

[72] *PH*, II, 204.
[73] *PH*, II, 195–198.

Sextus' doctrine of truth leads to essentially the same conclusion. Statements must be verifiable to be true, but no universal statement can be conclusively established by induction, since the particulars to which it refers are "countless and unlimited." Consequently, if such universal statements are used as premises in deductive arguments, the conclusions of these arguments are no less "shaky" than the premises, which is to say, neither the premises nor the conclusion can be regarded as true. Sextus' comments on induction demonstrate that he is quite aware that statements arrived at inductively cannot claim the certainty of deductive inferences. For this reason (and in accordance with his denial in other contexts that anything is true), he would reject the notion that such statements are true. Nevertheless, his criticism need not be taken as a repudiation of induction as such. To be sure, induction is unable to establish conclusively the truth of universal statements, thus destroying the certainty of conclusions deduced from them, when they are employed as premises in deductive arguments. Yet that is no objection against induction unless it is professed to yield absolutely certain results. If such a claim is not made, the argument quoted lacks force or is irrelevant. Sextus' own position indicates that he does not wish to abolish inductive procedures so much as to expose those who, while employing those procedures, cast the products of inductive inferences into the framework of a deductive system, thereby claiming absolute certainty for their results. Sextus, on the other hand, is at pains to make clear his own approval of the associative sign, the foundation of which, as he is doubtless aware, is induction. In doing so, therefore, he ends by divorcing the concepts of certainty and truth from the acceptable procedures of inference employed in life, namely, use of the associative sign (and induction), which he recommends as the only method to be employed as a basis for inferences to the unknown.

NOTHING IS TRUE. We have yet to inquire into Sextus' skeptical conclusions regarding truth. His empiricism, as we have seen, led to the view that statements must be verifiable in experience to be true. Statements about unobservable entities, therefore, as well as universal statements inductively arrived at, cannot be said to be true. In fact all perceptual statements, since they refer to external objects over and above phenomena, are ultimately excluded from the class of the true or false. On the other hand, his position does not appear to exclude sense statements from that class. Since a sense statement does not refer beyond phenomena, it would seem possible to refer it to the facts (phenomena, impressions) described and, consequently, to establish its truth or falsity. In spite of these considerations, Sextus declares unequivocally that nothing is true (οὐδέν ἐστιν ἀληθές).[74] Moreover, his declaration includes an explicit repudiation of the doctrine that "what convinces many"[75] is true, as well as the view of those who maintain that the "credible"[76] is true.

From the latter hypothesis, which is clearly that of Carneades, Sextus derives the contradiction that the same thing will be both true and false, since what is credible to one may not be credible to another. Furthermore, no matter how carefully experience (credible impressions) is tested, it may still be false. Proponents of the credible impression, Sextus concludes, are defeated by their own criticism. Arguing against the cataleptic impression, they insist there are other impressions, indistinguishable from it, which are false. But the same argument can be brought against the credible impression as a criterion of truth. Impressions can be scrutinized and subjected to many tests, but there will always be false ones indistinguishable from credible impressions. The possibility remains, therefore, that credible impressions, though they appear true, do not

---

[74] PH, II, 88 ff.; M, VIII, 17 ff.; 31 ff.
[75] M, VIII, 53–55; M, VII, 329; PH, II, 43–46.
[76] M, VIII, 51–53; VII, 435–439.

conform to their objects. On the other hand, Sextus charges, it is just "silly" (ληρῶδες) to say that whatever convinces many is true. This last arrow is probably aimed at Aenesidemus who, according to Sextus, held that phenomena common to all are true. On the contrary, Sextus maintains, the number of persons in agreement about phenomena has nothing to do with their truth.

> But even so, just as in the affairs of life it is not impossible for one intelligent person to be better than many unintelligent persons, so too in philosophy it is not unlikely for one person to possess good sense and for this reason to be trustworthy, but for many to be like geese and for this reason untrustworthy, even though they confirm in unison the testimony of the others about some matter.[77]

Commentary. Sextus' rejection of the doctrines of Carneades and Aenesidemus is instructive. He dismisses the credible impression as a standard of truth on the ground that, though such impressions appear true, they may (according to the Academic definition) in fact be false. This indicates that, for Sextus, the concepts of truth and certainty are inseparably linked — a connection that, as noted earlier, was abandoned by Carneades. The same conception of truth also accounts for his contemptuous attitude toward Aenesidemus' doctrine that phenomena about which there is general agreement are true. The fact of universal consent is no guarantee that the beliefs or experiences in question are true. Sextus makes clear his own position regarding the conditions necessary for claiming that phenomena are true. It must be possible to establish that those phenomena are identical with the real object.[78] And for this, a criterion of veridical experience is essential, which, as he has argued, is necessarily lacking.

---

[77] *M*, VII, 329. The context at *M*, VIII, 53–55 strongly suggests that Sextus has Aenesidemus in mind. The example of "that which convinces many" (τὸ πολλοὺς πεῖθον) is a phenomenon.

[78] *PH*, II, 88–89; *M*, VIII, 18–19.

Nevertheless, the implicit rejection of sense statements from the category of the true (and false) seems paradoxical for several reasons. First, truth, according to Sextus, is appropriate to statements; further, we are justified in saying how an object appears to us, though not what its real properties are; and finally, sense statements would very likely be regarded by Sextus as verifiable — a necessary condition for calling any statement true. Consider again the statement, "Honey appears sweet," which refers only to phenomena. If it is translated, "Honey appears sweet to me now," my own impressions are sufficient to establish its truth (or falsity, if I know, or come to discover, that the statement is not an accurate description of my experience). Or if the assertion means "Honey appears sweet to all (or most) persons" (though not implying in Sextus' case that the same phenomenon appears to all or most persons), it can be verified (confirmed) or falsified by consulting a sufficiently large number of persons concerning their respective experiences.[79]

That Sextus does not grant the truth or falsity of sense statements suggests an assumption on his part that the concept of truth can be appropriately employed only in connection with perceptual statements. That is, a statement, to be characterized as true or false, must first make a claim about some existing object (fact) in the world — must claim, for example, that something exists or has a certain character; we can then determine whether it is true by reference to the relevant objects or facts. Now a sense statement does not make such a claim; it says nothing about what exists or the character of existents. In keeping with the above assumption, then, the question of its truth or falsity would not arise. Accordingly, Sextus says that the word "criterion" has two main senses: that by which we judge reality and

---

[79] Whether or not verification (or confirmation) really would be possible on Sextus' view of the nature of experience is a complicated question. The point here is that Sextus would probably accept that sense statements can be established empirically.

unreality (ὕπαρξις καὶ ἀνυπαρξία), that is, the criterion of truth, and that which we use as a guide in ordinary life.[80] He thus links truth with the criterion by which we judge existence, and not with the criterion for the conduct of life. Sense statements descriptive of phenomena, which constitute the criterion for life, are therefore not likely to be thought of as true or false. Yet it is this very neutrality that makes them acceptable to Sextus. They are descriptive of our impressions, to which we are compelled by nature to grant assent. The Skeptics, he insists, do not abolish phenomena but accept them as a standard for life.[81] Of the two sorts of statement, the predicates "true" and "false" are applicable only to those that make claims about real existence. As a consequence, however, nothing is true. Sextus' skeptical conclusion is predicated in part on the assumption that any empirical statement that can be true or false makes a claim about a real external world — a domain that is, as he then proceeds to argue, completely unknown.

The above position, which by linking truth (and knowledge) with the real as opposed to the apparent conforms to a long tradition in Greek philosophical thought, can be seen more clearly by looking again at Sextus' objections to Acnesidemus' view of truth. Acnesidemus had asserted that some phenomena, namely, those appearing to all in common, are true. Sextus' criticism suggests a particular interpretation of that statement. He argues that truth and common opinion do not always coincide. It is not unusual for the majority to be wrong and the minority right in a particular controversy. Analogously, in the case of perception it is

----

[80] *PH*, II, 14–18; *M*, VII, 29–35. He goes on to say that the first sense of "criterion" has three meanings. He argues against only one of these, viz., "the logical," which is supposed to provide a standard for the apprehension of nonevident objects. The remaining two meanings are more general and pertain to "ordinary standards," such as the rule and compass and even the physical organs of sense. His main argument is thus with the philosophers.

[81] *PH*, I, 19, 21–22.

also possible that phenomena appearing to all in common are false. In order to maintain that some phenomena are true (and others false), we require a criterion of veridical experience, and for the reasons mentioned, common consent will not do. Underlying Sextus' objection is the assumption that true phenomena must be identical with the external object. That is, the force of his argument rests on the supposition that Aenesidemus is presenting a *criterion* for the truth of phenomena, the *conditions* of which have already been defined and agreed upon as the established identity of phenomenon with external object. For, of course, the numbers of persons sharing an experience will be of no help in determining whether such experiences conform to the object (whether the phenomena in question are identical with the object). Sextus is surely right on this point. Yet the statement of Aenesidemus is also suggestive of another line of thought, which Sextus does not follow up—he neither takes it to be Aenesidemus' meaning, nor does he incorporate the hint into his own thought. The assertion that phenomena appearing to all in common are true might be understood to provide a definition (necessary and sufficient conditions) of the truth of phenomena, rather than a criterion for deciding which phenomena are identical with real objects. And this train of reasoning leads ultimately to a change in application of the concept of truth, namely, to the view that sense statements can be true or false. To explore this possibility, let us for the moment suppose the second alternative to be the meaning of the statement in question. We can then say, roughly, that a phenomenon Y is true in relation to X if, and only if, X appears Y to all or most persons. For example, the phenomenon of sweetness is true in relation to honey if, and only if, honey appears sweet to all or most persons. But "the phenomenon of sweetness is true in relation to honey" can more easily be expressed by "'honey appears sweet' is true." Thus, we can say that "honey appears sweet" is true if, and only if, honey appears sweet to all or most persons, ending with something like conditions that define the truth of sense statements. Now it is clear that Sextus is not thinking along these lines. He does not interpret the position of Aenesidemus as providing a new definition of truth. Instead of taking the statement in question to provide a condition for the truth of "X appears Y," he sees it as furnishing a criterion (and a very poor one at that) for the truth of "X really is Y" — that is, for deciding whether phenomenon is identical with object. The assumption that truth must be connected with real existence, which Sextus apparently did not question, dictates that interpretation.

Sextus' conservatism with respect to the concept of truth is partly responsible for his skepticism. His position ends by barring the notion of truth from any application. For though the concept is properly applied to statements that make claims about real existence, on Sextus' view these statements turn out to be unverifiable, thus failing to fulfill an important condition of truth. He is forced to conclude, therefore, that nothing is true. Had Sextus not followed the tradition of assimilating the true to the real, a domain he believed to be unknowable in principle, he could have reclaimed the concept of truth by applying it to sense statements, which refer to phenomenal objects and hence are verifiable. The unknowable real object would thus have become quite superfluous. But Sextus rejects such a phenomenalistic position.[82] An object is more than an aggregate of its perceptible properties. The real object, as he has argued, exists independently of what we experience, whereas the phenomenal object is affected by the conditions and circumstances of perception. The idea of an object, therefore, is not exhausted by its phenomenal appearances. It is just this separation of external object and phenomenon, along with the association of truth with the real, which makes Sextus a skeptic instead of a phenomenalist.

[82] M, VII, 294–296.

Since nothing is true, however, it follows that not even the statements of the Skeptics themselves are true. Sextus acknowledges this inference, but the criticism is wide of the mark. The Skeptic doctrine is indeed self-refuting, but only after it has destroyed all the arguments of traditional philosophy.[83] Sextus sums up the Skeptic position in a passage following his arguments against the Stoic doctrine of demonstration.

> And again, just as it is not impossible for a man who has climbed up to a high place by a ladder to overturn the ladder with his foot after his ascent, so too it is not unreasonable that the Skeptic, after he has proceeded, as it were by a kind of ladder, to construct the above argument proving that there is no such thing as demonstration, should then also do away with this very argument.[84]

These conclusions recall the philosophy of Pyrrho, which Sextus' position resembles most closely. In denying that our sense experiences and beliefs are true or false, Pyrrho began a tradition of unqualified skepticism, which ultimately received its fullest expression in the philosophy of Sextus Empiricus.

---

[83] *PH*, I, 206; II, 188; *M*, VIII, 480; *Vit.*, IX, 76. Another way of meeting this type of objection was to remind the critic that Skeptic utterances are no more than reports of their own experiences, i.e., sense statements. Cf. *PH*, I, 15, 200.

[84] *M*, VIII, 481.

6 * CONCLUSION

The aim of the preceding chapters has been to set forth the Greek skeptical philosophies in as much detail as the information available to us permits. It is appropriate, in concluding, to consider these doctrines more generally in relation to the (logical) conditions in Greek philosophical thought which helped bring them about — viewing them as attempts to deal with, and perhaps provide solutions for, epistemological problems that beset the principal philosophical systems of the time — and also to reflect on the implications of Skepticism as they may be brought to bear on the substance of these same problems. We have seen that the skeptical philosophies are roughly of two main types. In keeping with the usual classification, this chapter views the doctrines of Pyrrhonists and Academic Skeptics as alternative ways of responding to epistemological problems inherent in a conceptual system consisting partly of presuppositions inherited from the philosophic tradition and partly of a new empiricism characteristic of the time. The conceptual framework provides a context within which the problems confronting Skeptics, and their treatment of these problems, are meaningful and of considerable philosophical interest.

To begin with, it has been observed more than once that a metaphysical distinction between phenomenal and real dominates Skepticism from its initial appearance in the fragments of Timon to its countless occurrences in the pages of Sextus Empiricus. This dualism permeates both Pyrrhonic and Academic Skepticism. It is explicit in the Pyrrhonic terms "phenomenon" and "external object" and more subtly present in the Academic distinction between conditions and criteria of truth. By the fourth century B.C. these categories had become a commonplace in Greek philosophical thinking, taken for granted and doubtless regarded as hardly in need of defending. But neither does such a philosophical assumption stand out as something to be consciously repudiated. The distinction was inherited by Skeptics from their philosophical predecessors, and it was accepted by them apparently without question. Though certain of their doctrines tend to undermine this distinction, as we shall see, it is by implication only and not by conscious intent.

A second feature, characteristic of Greek philosophical thought since Aristotle, is also common to the Skeptic philosophies examined. In answering the question of how we come to know the properties of the real world, Skeptics commit themselves to an important doctrine of empiricism. Knowledge of the real must originate in sensory experience. Reason has no direct insight into the nature of things, so that reality must be grasped indirectly, through the agency of the senses.[1] The word "experience" is, of course, ambiguous. We have remarked how terms, such as "sense experience" (αἴσθησις), "impression" (φαντασία), "affection" (πάθος), "phenomenon" (φαινόμενον), are variously employed by Skeptics in their accounts of the relation between knowledge and a minimal awareness of sensibles (αἰσθητά). The empirical analysis of sensory experience ends in a rep-

---

[1] The language employed by Skeptics suggests not only a sharp separation of sensory and intellective functions but often personification of these capacities (δυνάμεις). Cf., e.g., PH, I, 99, 128; II, 72; M, VII, 293–294, 344–347. This tends to dramatize the gap between phenomenon and real object by creating a picture, together with Skeptic empiricism, of mind the knower, shut off from the real world and therefore forced to get its information at second hand from the senses which, in any event, are able to grasp only sensibles. "For sense does not furnish the intellect with the external objects but only its own particular affection" (M, VII, 354). The old idea of an appropriate type of object corresponding to each distinct psychic faculty is badly cast with an empiricist epistemology, Aristotle notwithstanding.

resentative view of perception. A portion of our experience is true [2] (the real nature of an object is apprehended), only if the former is an exact replica of its object.

The Skeptic philosophies, therefore, must be viewed in the following context: The world has a dual character — its appearances and its real nature. We are acquainted through sense with the apparent, but in order to know, we must apprehend the real. The real properties of an object cannot be known independently of sense, however, since these objects are apprehended only through the media of impressions (affections). A necessary condition of knowing is that our impressions be exact likenesses of the object to which they correspond. The main problem to which Skeptics addressed themselves concerned a criterion of truth to facilitate differentiating decisively between veridical and nonveridical experience. Accordingly, the question that required an answer was how we can be sure that our experience of an object is an exact copy of it. And the Skeptic reply was that we cannot be sure. There is no way to establish this relation. Skepticism is an authentic response to the problem of knowledge as it arose within the above context, that is, within a conceptual framework that helped generate a problem for which, as the Skeptics saw, there was no solution.

The Academic and Pyrrhonic philosophies represent alternative ways of coping with their similar conclusions concerning the impossibility of knowing (being certain of) the character of the real world. Academics reacted to this predicament by giving up the ideal of certainty with respect to perceptual assertions. Putting aside the question of how we can be certain of the truth of experiences and beliefs, they concentrated on the related one of justifying assent. No perceptual statement

---

[2] There is no consistency among Skeptics over use of the term "true." It is employed with reference to "experiences and beliefs" by Pyrrho, "impressions" by Carneades, "phenomena" by Aenesidemus, and "statements" by Sextus Empiricus.

(or belief) can be guaranteed, but there are reasons for accepting some statements as true and rejecting others as false. The Academic philosophy is an attempt to formulate criteria of truth based on tests other than that of comparing experience with its object. Carneades' criteria specify that credible (consistent, tested) experience is sufficient to warrant a perceptual assertion. Qualified assent is given to an assertion when it is supported by evident experience, and disagreements of fact can be settled on the same basis. In brief, the criteria determine what counts as acceptable ground for a perceptual statement and what can be adduced as justification for such a claim, though they cannot assure the truth of any perceptual utterance or belief. In changing the direction of their inquiry to the question of justification and detaching the procedure of justifying a perceptual statement from the problem of matching impressions against their objects, Academic Skeptics thus sought a way out of the difficulties that their philosophic criticism had brought to light. By changing the subject they did not, of course, solve the original problem. But such a shift in emphasis may be regarded as symptomatic of a need to restate the problem of knowledge in such a way as not to preclude at the outset a solution to it.

Pyrrhonists, on the other hand, reacted differently to the results of their skeptical criticism. If, as they contended, we cannot be certain of the real properties of things, we ought not to concern ourselves with such matters but suspend judgment instead. Investigations into the real nature of things are necessarily speculative and cannot be anchored to the facts of experience. They maintained further that philosophic speculation is not necessary to manage the affairs of everyday life but is even antithetical to happiness or ataraxia.[3] The Pyrrhonist is guided by phenomena, which (though they do not yield knowledge) provide a criterion for the conduct of life. In the course of showing that assertions

[3] *PH*, I, 25–31.

about the real properties of objects are unfounded, Pyrrhonists suggest a way in which epistemological questions might be dealt with on a purely phenomenal level. Since the object of perception is the phenomenon and not a reality beyond it, claims about external objects are not justified. These entities either cannot be perceived, or if perceptible, they cannot be compared with phenomenal objects. Statements descriptive of phenomena, however, have the authority of experience behind them. The Skeptic does not (indeed cannot) deny the facts of his own experience to which he is naturally compelled to assent. Assertions that do no more than report correctly these experienced data are therefore acceptable (justified). There is in this case, as already noted, no problem of matching experience against object. Further, the concept of truth can be applied to phenomena in such a way as to distinguish phenomena that appear to all alike from the rest. By extending the notion of general agreement to philosophical method and adding the doctrine of the associative sign as a basis for inference about the nonevident, Pyrrhonists suggest a conception of explanation appropriate only to phenomena. If philosophical doctrines are to be explanatory of phenomena, they must derive their evidence from phenomena and enable us to draw inferences about phenomena that are temporarily nonevident. The Pyrrhonic criticism effects a shift of attention from the real but hidden nature of things to their phenomenal characteristics, which can be observed.

Let us return to the antithesis between the real world and its appearances, which has been stressed as a significant factor in shaping Greek skeptical philosophies. Although there is no evidence that Skeptics openly called this assumption into question, there is reason to conclude that a covert effect of both Pyrrhonism and Academic Skepticism is logically to undermine this traditional distinction.

The effect is most readily seen in connection with the Academic philosophy. Unlike the Pyrrhonists, Aca-

demics maintained that the external object (if anything)
is what is perceived. It is the real object that is grasped,
even if with insufficient clarity to warrant assent. This
has special significance with respect to the appearance-
reality dichotomy which, though present in the Academic distinction between "apparently true" and "true"
(criteria and conditions of truth), does not extend to the
substantives "appearances" and "external (real) object."
We do not perceive appearances of an object but the
object itself and, hence, the existent. Two consequences
follow. First, the traditional linking of knowledge with
the real and sense experience (and belief) with the apparent is broken. Knowing and believing (holding an
opinion) are distinguished not by their objects but only
by the degree of certainty accruing to them. To be sure,
knowledge (certainty) is impossible, but we are not
barred from (a lesser) apprehension of the real in ordinary perceptual experience. A second and related consequence is that there are no additional entities to be
contrasted with the existing objects of perception. Academics thought it correct to distinguish conceptually
between "true" and "apparently true," but they did
not, in parallel fashion, contrast the existing object
with its appearances. The effect is to neutralize the
ontological dualism between apparent and real, since
there are no longer two kinds of things in the world,
or two ontological levels, but only one.

But even Pyrrhonism, with its more orthodox association of knowledge with the existent and sense experience (and belief) with the apparent, ends by subverting the same distinction, if in a less obvious way. This
can be seen by reflecting on what we may call the "paradox of Pyrrhonism" — the contention that Pyrrhonism
is consistent with ordinary life.

We find Pyrrhonists as early as Timon and as late as
Sextus Empiricus professing that their philosophy does
not conflict with the beliefs and practices of ordinary life.
Timon "denies that he has gone beyond ordinary cus-

tom."[4] The implications seen by Aenesidemus in the
word "true" ("that which does not escape common
opinion")[5] suggest compatibility with ordinary beliefs;
and Sextus sometimes even adds the claim that Pyrrhonists are the advocates of common sense.[6] In the following passage Sextus sums up the Pyrrhonic position
most characteristically.

> For it is sufficient, I think, to live by experience, and with-
> out subscribing to beliefs, according to common practices
> and preconceptions, suspending judgment with respect to
> those statements that issue from dogmatic subtlety and are
> furthest removed from the usage of ordinary life.[7]

This passage brings to mind the doctrines of both
Pyrrho and Aenesidemus by recommending a life without beliefs (ἀδοξάστως) but in accordance with "common"
(κοιναί) preconceptions, and by urging suspense of judgment with respect to those statements that depart
furthest from ordinary life

But there is a paradox implicit in these recommendations and in the suggestion that Pyrrhonism is compatible with common sense beliefs. How can the Pyrrhonist
claim not to have departed from ordinary life? His investigations seem to have led to some quite unorthodox
conclusions. The repudiation of perceptual statements
as a class is on the face of it a clear violation of ordinary
usage. The distinction drawn between real objects,
which are unknown, and their appearances, which are
perceived but furnish no information about the real,
seems also to clash with common sense. It is at least
questionable whether ordinary conceptions include the
belief that sweetness is not a real property of honey or
that investigations into the real properties of an object

[4] *Poet.*, frag. 81.
[5] *M*, VIII, 8.
[6] *PH*, II, 102; *M*, VIII, 158.
[7] *PH*, II, 246: ἀρκεῖ γάρ, οἶμαι, τὸ ἐμπείρως τε καὶ ἀδοξάστως κατὰ
τὰς κοινὰς τηρήσεις τε καὶ προλήψεις βιοῦν, περὶ τῶν ἐκ δογματικῆς
περιεργίας καὶ μάλιστα ἔξω τῆς βιωτικῆς χρείας λεγομένων ἐπέχοντας.

transcend experience. The solution to this puzzle lies in the nature of the Pyrrhonic contrast between external object and phenomenon.

The point of the distinction is to draw attention to the fact that our experience is affected by different conditions and circumstances under which something is perceived. The world as it is experienced is in part a product of the very conditions under which perception takes place. This seems a perfectly legitimate observation. It would be difficult to maintain, to the contrary, that the conditions of perception have no effect on its content. Analogously, sense statements are contrasted with perceptual statements to mark off assertions about objects that can be experienced from those about the unperceivable. The Pyrrhonist's acceptance of sense statements and his repudiation of perceptual statements constitute an implicit recommendation to limit our claims about the world to those things falling within the range of experience. This too is not an unreasonable request. Pyrrhonism seems to forsake common sense, however, by denying knowledge of the real character of an object and claiming awareness only of its apparent properties. The recommendation to translate perceptual statements into sense statements at this point becomes a proposal to talk about the appearances of things instead of the objects themselves. An unconditioned (or unidentifiable) object is identified with the real and the perceptual object with its appearances. The transition can be justified only if statements about the real (perceptual statements) are in fact assertions about such an unknowable object. Here we have a clue to the perplexing claim that Pyrrhonism is consistent with ordinary life.

The Pyrrhonic arguments are intended to demonstrate the futility of attempts to grasp a reality that transcends appearances and thereby to guard against perceptual claims pertaining to that unknowable domain. It is important to determine what bearing the conclusion of these arguments, that we can say how an object appears but not what its real properties are, has on the statements of ordinary life. Two characteristic features of common sense assertions are especially relevant to this question. It is noteworthy, first, that ordinary statements of fact are (often) about existing things (facts) as contrasted with appearances and, second, that they are concerned to make claims about objects as perceived and not about entities that might exist independently of all perceptual conditions. If someone remarks that honey is sweet, he is not ascribing a property to an entity that cannot enter into, or be identified as part of, his experience. He is talking about something that is experienced and asserting that this object has a certain flavor. But neither is he prepared for this reason to admit to assigning a property to an appearance of honey. We have seen that such ordinary statements of fact cannot falsify the Pyrrhonist's claim that we can legitimately make claims only about the appearances of an object and not about the object itself. If someone should maintain that an object, which appears yellow in this light, really is white, his assertion is, in an important sense, irrelevant to the Skeptic conclusion, because the distinction between things and their appearances, when it is made in ordinary circumstances, is not the philosophic distinction between an object untouched by perceptual conditions and a perceived object. But by the same token the Skeptic contention has a peculiarly irrelevant ring when taken in the context of common sense assertions. For they do not purport to disclose the character of an object that cannot be (identified as) a component of the speaker's experience but only to characterize something that is (can be) perceived. What, then, is the man who says that honey is sweet talking *about* — phenomenon or external object? It is not clear how to answer this question, for he doubtless would not refer to it either way. The object designated by "honey," the name actually employed, does not readily fit either classification. It is something perceived, but it is also believed to exist (to be real) and to have properties that remain stable under varying perceptual conditions. The contention that we can describe appearances but not real characteristics is difficult to apply to common sense assertions, because the distinction between phenomenon and external object, to which the Skeptic arguments call our attention, does not correspond to any distinction in ordinary usage. This accounts for the fact that common sense assertions cannot counter the Skeptic conclusion and also for what seems to be a genuine (but not total) irrelevance of that conclusion to ordinary beliefs or statements.

The reason for the irrelevance felt in this regard is, as already noted, that the real object, which is said to be unknowable, is not (identifiable as) any of the familiar objects of our experience. The Skeptic conclusion thus gives us no information about these experienced objects, including whether or not they can be known. The intended force of the Skeptic arguments is to make the point that the objects familiar to us are in fact phenomena. But this is to say (in part) that they are perceptual objects and not something over and above what is perceived. Since common sense assertions, despite their formulation as perceptual statements and not sense statements, make no claims about transcendent entities, they are in this respect untouched by the Skeptic conclusion. On the other hand, the Pyrrhonist's argument is not completely irrelevant to common sense beliefs, because phenomenal objects do not remain unaltered under varying perceptual conditions. His argument informs us, therefore, that whatever properties the objects of our experience may have, they are in some measure determined by the conditions under which perception takes place. The ordinary person, though he is ready to grant that his experience is affected by perceptual conditions — that the white object may look yellow in a certain light — is also prepared to maintain that the character of the object itself is unaffected by varying conditions of perception. That is, he is inclined to assume that, though the object may *look* different in other circumstances, its *real* properties remain the same. In this connection the Pyrrhonist has pointed out that what we usually think of as the "real" properties are only those perceived under certain conditions, which, though generally accepted, cannot be established as disclosing the real nature of the object Hence his conclusion, neutralizing the conventional dis tinction between the real and apparent, tells us that in no case of perception can we say more than how an object appears. The implication of the Skeptic argument, therefore, is to say that we are justified in thinking of objects and their characteristics only in a perceptual context that plays a role in determining these characteristics. We cannot with consistency hold the belief that the character of the perceptual object itself is unaffected by the conditions under which it is perceived. In this respect the Skeptic position seems to conflict with common sense beliefs. And if it is incompatible with them, it cannot be irrelevant to them.

The conflict, however, appears not to be in ordinary perceptual assertions as such. They do not, as we have seen, purport to assign properties to transcendent objects, and for this reason they are uncontradicted by the Skeptic conclusion. Consider again the Pyrrhonist's example "Honey is sweet." The object referred to on the usual occasions of such an utterance is an identifiable object of experience, to which a trait that is or can be experienced is assigned. The assertion therefore is not incompatible with the Skeptic unwillingness to countenance statements about real (transcendent) objects. But it is also important to note that the assertion in itself does not tell us anything about the speaker's beliefs concerning the object honey — whether or not it is regarded as a *phenomenal* object. If the speaker believes, assumes, or takes it for granted that the property of sweetness is an invariant characteristic of honey, irrespective of the presence or absence of what the Skeptic would take to be a relevant set of perceptual conditions, then the Skeptic position conflicts, not with his perceptual statement, but with these assumptions or beliefs that he entertains about the perceptual object. The Skeptic arguments urge us to view the objects of experience not as entities isolated from a perceptual context but as objects whose features are intimately connected with, indeed inseparable from, this context. The conflict between Pyrrhonism and common sense lies in the fact that the ordinary person is not likely to do this. But it does not lie in his perceptual assertions about those objects, which are incompatible with the Skeptic conclusion in form only. Translation into the corresponding sense statement ("Honey appears sweet to X") in such cases would merely function as a reminder of the relevance of the subject himself to the character of the object as it is perceived by him — a reminder that the object in question is a phenomenal object.

It was mentioned earlier that the difficulty in relating the Skeptic position to the statements of ordinary life arises out of the absence of a common sense distinction corresponding to that between the Pyrrhonic phenomenon and external object. This is not without significance. For the distinction between a (necessarily) hidden reality and its manifest appearances, if not a recognizable one in ordinary discourse, is readily available in philosophical discourse. It is embedded in most of the systems of Greek philosophers, with respect to which the Skeptic arguments are, as it happens, especially relevant. In view of this fact, and the Pyrrhonist's claim not to have violated ordinary beliefs and practices, it is reasonable to conclude that his arguments are not intended to challenge the assertions of ordinary life so much as to launch an attack on philosophical theories, which after drawing the distinction in question claim to disclose the real but hidden nature of things as contrasted with their manifest appearances.[8] Accordingly, Sextus

---

[8] This is never made quite clear in the Skeptic writings, which helps to explain the difficulties encountered in determining the

Empiricus speaks contemptuously of philosophers who, in an effort to refute arguments purporting to prove, for example, that snow is black or that motion is impossible, hasten to invent others to reassure us that snow really is white or that objects really do move.[9] All that is necessary to expose such "nonsense" is the evidence of experience (phenomena).

> Thus, in fact, a certain philosopher, when asked about the argument against motion, silently began to walk about, and ordinary persons set out on journeys on foot and by sea and build ships and houses and produce children without paying any attention to the arguments against motion and generation.[10]

The Pyrrhonist's claim that we can give an account only of appearances is aimed at those whose doctrines thus violate common sense. To limit inquiry and discussion to phenomena is simply to confine investigation to objects as they are perceived. And this amounts to a proposal to be guided by common sense. Pyrrhonism, in its opposition to traditional philosophy, is therefore consistent with ordinary life. But to the extent that it is compatible with common sense beliefs, it is also subversive of the philosophical dichotomy between a real object and its appearances. Ordinary usage does not distinguish between a transcendent object and a perceptual object. Philosophers have invented these categories, identifying an unperceivable entity with the existent and the perceived with its appearances. Consequently, if Pyrrhonism is intended to attack philosophical theories about the real nature of things, it has

---

force of their arguments. But there are many suggestions to that effect, e.g., as found in the quotation that follows (cf. also chap. 4, n. 29). Granting that the Skeptic assertions are intended to challenge the statements of philosophers rather than those of ordinary men, we still cannot say to what extent Sextus, for example, was aware (if at all) of the irrelevance of the Pyrrhonist's conclusion to common sense (perceptual) assertions.

[9] *PH*, II, 244.
[10] *Ibid.*

the effect logically of weakening the power of those traditional concepts. Pyrrhonism, though itself a product of the dualism between the real and its appearances, ends by subtly undermining this very distinction.

BIBLIOGRAPHY

TEXTS, TRANSLATIONS, AND COMMENTARIES

Arnim, Hans von. *Stoicorum Veterum Fragmenta*. Leipzig: Teubner, 1905–1924.

Athenaeus. *The Deipnosophists*. Trans. C. B. Gulick. Loeb Classical Library. Vols. 2–4. London: Heinemann, 1928–1930. Vol. 5. Cambridge: Harvard University Press, 1955.

Augustine, St. *Against the Academics*. Trans. John J. O'Meara. Westminster, Md.: Newmann, 1950.

——. *Answer to Skeptics*. Trans. D. J. Kavanagh. New York: Cosmopolitan Science and Art, 1943.

Cicero. *De Finibus*. Trans. H. Rackham. Loeb Classical Library. London: Heinemann; Cambridge: Harvard University Press, 1951.

——. *De Natura Deorum; Academica*. Trans. H. Rackham. Loeb Classical Library. London: Heinemann; Cambridge: Harvard University Press, 1956.

——. *De Oratore*. Trans. H. Rackham. Loeb Classical Library. London: Heinemann, Cambridge: Harvard University Press, 1960.

Deichgräber, Karl. *Die griechische Empirikerschule*. Berlin: Weidmann, 1930.

Diels, Hermann. *Die Fragmente der Vorsokratiker*. Ed. W. Kranz. 9th ed. Berlin; Weidmann, 1959–1960.

——. *Doxographi Graeci*. 3d ed. Berlin: De Gruyter, 1958.

——. *Poetarum Philosophorum Fragmenta*. Vol. 3, no. 1, in *Poetarum Graecorum Fragmenta*. Ed. U. von Wilamowitz-Moellendorff. Berlin: Weidmann, 1901.

Diogenes Laertius. *Lives of Eminent Philosophers*. Trans. R. D. Hicks. Loeb Classical Library. London: Heinemann; Cambridge: Harvard University Press, 1958–1959. 2 vols.

——. *Vitae Philosophorum*. Ed. C. Cobet. Paris: Firmin-Didot, 1878.

Eusebius. *Praeparatio Evangelica*. Ed. E. H. Gifford. Oxford: Oxford University Press, 1903.

Gellius, Aulus. *The Attic Nights of Aulus Gellius*. Trans. J. C. Rolfe. Loeb Classical Library. London: Heinemann; Cambridge: Harvard University Press. Vols. 2–3, 1948–1952.

Mullach, F. W. A. *Fragmenta Philosophorum Graecorum*. Paris: Firmin-Didot, 1881.

Photius. *Bibliotheca*. Ed. I. Bekker. Berlin: Reimer, 1824.
Plutarch. *Moralia*. Ed. G. N. Bernardakis. Leipzig: Teubner, 1896–1908.
Reid, James S. M. *Tulli Ciceronis Academica*. London: Macmillan, 1885.
Sextus Empiricus. *Opera*. Ed. H. Mutschmann. Vols. 1, 2 (1912–1914); Ed. Mau (Index, Janacek). Vol. 3 (1954). Leipzig: Teubner, 1912–1954.
————. *Scepticism, Man and God: Selections from the Major Writings of Sextus Empiricus*. Ed. Phillip Hallie. Trans. Sanford Etheridge. Middletown, Conn: Wesleyan University Press, 1964.
————. *Sextus Empiricus*. Trans. R. G. Bury. Loeb Classical Library. London: Heinemann; Cambridge: Harvard University Press, 1949–1957. 4 vols.
Strabo. *The Geography of Strabo*. Trans. H. L. Jones. Loeb Classical Library. London: Heinemann; New York: Putnam; Cambridge: Harvard University Press. Vol. 1, 1949; Vol. 4, 1954; Vol. 8, 1949.
Suidas. *Lexicon*. Ed. I. Bekker. Berlin: Reimer, 1854.
Vogel, C. J. de. *Greek Philosophy*. Leiden: Brill, 1953–1959.
Walzer, R. *Galen on Medical Experience*. London, New York, Toronto: Oxford University Press, 1944.
Wilamowitz-Moellendorff, U. von. *Antigonos von Karystos*. Vol. 4, *Philologische Untersuchungen*. Ed. Kiessling and Wilamowitz-Moellendorff. Berlin: Weidmann, 1881.

CRITICAL STUDIES

Arnim, Hans von. "Arkesilaos," Pauly-Wissowa, *Realencyclopädie der classischen Altertumswissenschaft*, 2, no. 1 (Stuttgart: Metzler, 1895), 1164–1168.
————. "Karneades," Pauly-Wissowa, *Realencyclopädie der classischen Altertumswissenschaft*, 10, no. 2 (Stuttgart: Druckenmuller, 1919), 1964–1985.
Arnold, E. V. *Roman Stoicism*. Cambridge: Cambridge University Press, 1911.
Beare, J. I. *Greek Theories of Elementary Cognition from Alcmaeon to Aristotle*. Oxford: Clarendon, 1906.
Bevan, Edwin. *Stoics and Sceptics*. Oxford: Clarendon, 1913.
Bréhier, Émile. *Études de Philosophie Antique*. Paris: Presses Universitaires de France, 1955.
Brochard, Victor. *Les Sceptiques Grecs*. 2d ed. reprinted. Paris: Librairie Philosophique J. Vrin, 1959.
Broeker, W. "Die Tropen der Skeptiker," *Hermes*, 86 (1958), 497–499.
Bury, R. G. "Timon Fragments 65 and 67," *Proceedings of the Cambridge Philological Society*, 163–165 (1936), 5.
Chisholm, Roderick. "Sextus Empiricus and Modern Empiricism," *Philosophy of Science*, 8, no. 3 (1941), 371–384.
————. *Theory of Knowledge*. Englewood Cliffs, N. J.: Prentice-Hall, 1966.

Couissin, P. "L'Origine et l'évolution de l'ἐποχή," *Revue des Études Grecques*, 42 (1929), 373–397.

DeLacy, Estelle. "Meaning and Methodology in Hellenistic Philosophy," *Philosophical Review*, 47 (1938), 390–409.

DeLacy, Phillip. "οὐ μᾶλλον and the Antecedents of Ancient Scepticism," *Phronesis*, 3, no. 1 (1958), 59–71.

———. "Plutarch and the Academic Sceptics," *Classical Journal* 49, no. 2 (1953), 79–85.

Frenkian, A. M. *Scepticismul grec si filozofia indiana*. Bucuresti: Editura Populare Romine, 1957. Includes summaries in French and Russian. Substantially the same work appears in German in *Bibliotheca Classica Orientalis*, 4 (1958), 211–250.

Gigon, O. "Zur Geschichte der sogennanten Neuen Akademie," *Museum Helveticum* (1944), 47–64.

Goedeckemeyer, A. *Die Geschichte des griechischen Skeptizismus*. Leipzig: Welcher, 1905.

Heath, Thomas. *A History of Greek Mathematics*. Oxford: Clarendon, 1921.

Heintz, Werner. *Studien zu Sextus Empiricus*. Ed. Richard Harder. Halle: Niemeyer, 1932.

Hicks, R. D. *Stoic and Epicurean*. New York: Scribner, 1910.

Janacek, Karel. "Prolegomena to Sextus Empiricus," *Acta Universitatis Palackianae Olomucensis*, 4 (1948), 64 pp.

———. "Sextus Empiricus en der Arbeit," *Philologus*, 100 (1956), 100 107.

Maccoll, Norman. *The Greek Sceptics*. London and Cambridge: Macmillan, 1869.

Mates, Benson. *Stoic Logic*. 2d print. Berkeley and Los Angeles: University of California Press, 1961.

——— "Stoic Logic and the Text of Sextus Empiricus," *American Journal of Philology*, 70, no. 3 (1949), 290–298.

Minar, E. L. "The Positive Beliefs of the Skeptic Carneades," *Classical Weekly*, 43, no. 5 (1949), 67–71.

More, P. E. *Hellenistic Philosophies*. Princeton: Princeton University Press, 1923.

Mutschmann, H. "Die Stufen der Wahrscheinlichkeit bei Karneades," *Rheinisches Museum für Philologie*, LXVI (1911), 190–198.

———. "Die Überlieferung der Schriften des Sextus Empiricus," *Rheinisches Museum für Philologie*, LXIV (1909), 244–283.

Natorp, Paul. *Forschungen zu Geschichte des Erkenntnis Problems im Alterthum*. Berlin: Hertz, 1884.

Patrick, Mary Mills. *The Greek Sceptics*. New York: Columbia University Press, 1929.

———. *Sextus Empiricus and Greek Scepticism*. Cambridge: Bell, 1899.

Popkin, Richard. "Berkeley and Scepticism," *Review of Metaphysics*, 5, no. 2 (1951), 223–246.

———. "David Hume: His Pyrrhonism and His Critique of Pyrrhonism," *Philosophical Quarterly*, 1, no. 5 (1951), 385–407.

————. *The History of Scepticism from Erasmus to Descartes.* Assen: Van Gorcum, 1960.

Richards, H. "Varia" (Timon), *Classical Review,* 21 (1907), 197–199.

Robin, L. *Pyrrhon et Le Scepticisme Grec.* Paris: Presses Universitaires de France, 1944.

Roeper, Gottlieb. "Zu Laertios Diogenes I," *Philologus,* 30 (1870), 557–577.

Saisset, Emile. *Le Scepticisme.* 2d ed. Paris: Didier, 1865.

Sandbach, F. G. "ἔννοια and πρόληψις in Stoic Theory," *Classical Quarterly,* 24, no. 1 (1930), 44–51.

Shorey, Paul. "Emendation of Sextus Empiricus πρὸς γραμματικούς 126," *Classical Philology,* 10, no. 2 (1915), 218–219.

————. "Notes on Sextus Empiricus πρὸς μουσικούς 21," *Classical Philology,* 11, no. 1 (1916), 99.

Wellmann, Max. "Die empirische Schule," Pauly-Wissowa, *Realencyclopädie der classichen Altertumswissenschaft,* 5, no. 2 (Stuttgart: Metzler, 1905), 2516–2524.

Zeller, Eduard. *Die Philosophie der Griechen.* 5th ed. Leipzig: Reisland, 1922.

————. *History of Eclecticism in Greek Philosophy.* Trans. S. F. Alleyne. London: Longmans, Green, 1883.

————. *Plato and the Older Academy.* Trans. S. F. Alleyne and A. Goodwin. 3d ed. New York: Russell and Russell, 1962.

————. *Socrates and the Socratic Schools.* Trans. O. J. Reichel. 3d ed. New York: Russell and Russell, 1962.

————. *Stoics, Epicureans, and Sceptics.* Trans. O. J. Reichel. London: Longmans, Green, 1880.

INDEX